WHAT OTHERS ARE SAYING...

"What a wonderful book! Drawing on her personal experience, thorough research, and personal intuitive skills, Karen Felix has written an important book on the "bending" of Christian values to perpetuate racism, power, and privilege. This book is an important contemporary chapter in the search for understanding of how our faith has been exploited and includes specific steps we can take to advance love and social equity."

—Lee Morgan
President, *Morgan Family Foundation*
Social Justice Advocate

"Dr. Karen Felix-Neal's passionate heart cry against social justice hypocrisy is an indictment and rebuke against the Church for which Jesus gave His life. She calls for brothers and sisters in Christ, regardless of skin color, to stop calling evil good and good evil and to bring reconciliation to the body of Christ by means of the Gospel. We must wake up, see the destruction and division caused by social justice hypocrisy, and repent, bringing love not hate, healing not hurt, glorifying God not man, so we can once again restore unity to Christ's body."

—Dr. B .H. Smith
Founder and Chancellor of *Christ Power and Wisdom Bible Institute*, Delaware

"Dr. Karen Felix-Neal's *To My White Evangelical Brothers and Sisters with Love* will challenge your perception of three stark realities that influence our daily lives: racism, politics and religion. A must-read for anyone who wants to understand the Evangelical movement and how it has altered American society, especially its effect during the current presidential administration. Karen's conviction to warn is evident, and her passion to see all free from sin and death is revealed."

—W. Jackson
Pastor and Author
A Higher Dimension Church, Delaware

"*To My White Evangelical Brothers and Sisters with Love* is bold, truthful, and painful in many ways. This book is a clear wakeup call to all Christians who believe they are not prejudiced and/or feel they are right in their own eyes."

—L. M. Robinson

"In *To My White Evangelical Brothers and Sisters with Love,* Dr. Pastor Karen Felix-Neal addresses systemic racism, one of America's hidden secrets, with passion, wisdom, and understanding. This timely message is well delivered and should be read not only by believers but today's youth also."

—C. R. Long
President, *JeJaJo Travel & Tours* LLC

"As oldest sister to Rev. Dr. Karen Neal-Felix, I have attempted to read this book without bias and realized it was impossible. I'm just so proud of the body of work she has laid before us as she candidly shares God's Word and her experiences so others can apply what she has learned."

—D. Slaton
Licensed MSW, CRC Church, Georgia

"God speaks to Dr Karen Felix Neal in numerous dreams and visions, and she heard from the Lord on this one! *To My White Evangelical Brothers and Sisters with Love* reveals the uncomfortable truth of racism in America that must be exposed. To all Evangelicals, especially our Caucasian brothers and sisters who follow Jesus Christ, I highly recommend reading this book and keeping in your Christian history library. May God turn your heart back to the Father."

—Minister G. M.
Dominguez, Alabama

"Dr Karen Felix is a prophetess who operates in dreams and interpretation. So many have come true, I am in awe as she tells me what they mean. You owe it to yourself and others to experience this amazing gift God has given her."

—Rev. Dr. G. C. Neal III
Senior Pastor, A Higher Dimension Church, Delaware

"Our Lord knows what this world needs, and *To My White Evangelical Brothers and Sisters with Love* is a book the world needs at such a time as this. Our White Evangelical brothers and sisters need to hear what the Spirit is saying. I can't wait to hold a printed copy in my hand, as I know quite a few people I'd like to read this book."

—U. A.
CEO Caleb Investments

"Karen is a seer who has been given a spiritual gift of having and interpreting prophetic dreams, otherwise known as a "watchman in the spirit." Many of these dreams have already come true. Some are happening now. Some will be happening in the near future. Karen has seen the White Evangelical church being deceived by Satan himself, and God has asked her to share her dreams and interpretation with them. As God assured the "watchman on the wall" (Ezekiel 33), if they don't listen, the blood will not be on her hands."

—Anonymous

TO MY WHITE BROTHERS AND SISTERS WITH LOVE

A Black Evangelical Heart-Cry
Against Social Justice Hypocrisy
within the White Evangelical Church

DR. KAREN T. FELIX-NEAL

HDDD Publishing
Middletown, Delaware
USA

Copyright © 2020 by Karen T. Felix-Neal

ISBN 978-0-578-77555-5

HDBD Publishing
Middletown, DE

Visit author's website at **drfelixthewatchman.com**.

Publisher's Cataloging-in-Publication Data

Names: Felix-Neal, Karen T., author.

Title: To my white brothers and sisters with love : a Black evangelical heart-cry against social justice hypocrisy within the white evangelical church / by Dr. Karen T. Felix-Neal.

Description: Middletown, DE: HDBD Publishing, 2020.

Identifiers: LCCN: 2020918899 | ISBN: 9780578775555

Subjects: LCSH Race relations--Religious aspects--Christianity. | Racism--Religious aspects--Christianity. | Reconciliation--Religious aspects--Christianity. | Evangelicalism. | Racism--United States--History--21st century. | African Americans--Social conditions--21st century. | BISAC RELIGION / Christian Living / Social Issues

Classification: LCC BT734.2 .F45 2020 | DDC 277.3/083089--dc23

1 3 5 7 9 10 8 6 4 2

Printed in the United States of America

DEDICATION

To my husband Gaylord and daughters Gerri and Autumn, my heartbeats.

ACKNOWLEDGEMENTS

I give honor and praise to **my Heavenly Father, my Lord and Savior Jesus Christ, and the Holy Spirit**. I am nothing and can do nothing without the Trinity. I depend on You, Lord, for my total being, existence, and anything that is positive in me. I pray that this work is pleasing to You and I give all honor and glory to You. My prayer is that I'm fulfilling Your purpose as one of Your watchmen and blowing Your trumpet in accordance to the words You have given me.

I thank my pastor, **Dr. Belinda Smith**, for allowing the Holy Spirit to guide you in all your teachings, unselfish love, guidance, and inspiration! I would not be writing this message without you encouraging me.

I thank my siblings, **Debbie**, **Lisa**, **Rodd**, **Gail**, **Tina**, and **Jonathan**, for their unconditional love and support and for truly loving me with the love of Jesus Christ.

I give special thanks to and have been deeply blessed by the steadfast love and support of my husband, **Rev. Dr. Gaylord Neal**, and my daughters, **Gerri** and **Autumn**. I love them more than words can convey.

I also thank my White Sister in Christ, **Jeanette Windle**, without whose assistance this project would not have come to fruition. Not only did she use her God-gifting of editing, but her insightful critique was invaluable to this project.

TABLE OF CONTENTS

INTRODUCTION

A WATCHMAN ON THE WALL

As you read this book, please understand it is not intended as an angry diatribe against a group of people I resent, blame, or hate. I am not an activist of any sort nor a proponent of any particular political party. I am not trying to win an argument with anyone. I am certainly not a "leftist."

On the contrary, I came to Christ and have spent my adult life within the Evangelical movement. As a Black Evangelical Christian, I have personally encountered racism within and outside the church. But I have also been mentored and befriended by countless Evangelical Christians who are White. The overwhelming emotion I feel toward my White Evangelical brothers and sisters is love. Christ's love.

That said, God has laid on my heart a strong word of caution I feel impelled by the Holy Spirit to share with my White Evangelical brethren. More than twenty-five hundred years ago, God gave a stern warning to the prophet Ezekiel, who was His voice to a rebellious people of Israel when they were in captivity for their sins in Babylon.

The word of the Lord came to me: "Son of man, speak to your people and say to them, If I bring the sword upon a land, and the people of the land take a man from among them, and make him their watchman, and if he sees the sword coming upon the land and blows the trumpet and warns the people, then if anyone who hears the sound of the trumpet does not take warning, and the sword comes and takes him away, his blood shall be upon his own head . . . But if the watchman sees the sword coming and does not blow the trumpet, so that the people are not warned, and the sword comes and takes any one of them, that person is taken away in his iniquity, but his blood I will require at the watchman's hand. So you, son of man, I have made a watchman for the house of Israel. Whenever you hear a word from my mouth, you shall give them warning from me." (Ezekiel 33:1-8, ESV).

In summary, God told Ezekiel that if as His watchman God sent a warning of impending danger and Ezekiel faithfully passed on that warning, then any listeners who chose to ignore the warning would suffer the consequences, but the watchman would be held blameless. Conversely, if the watchman received God's warning but chose not to pass it on, the watchman would be held equally guilty of blood spilled.

The spiritual gift God has given me is that of prophecy and vision. And as with Ezekiel, God has laid on my heart a strong warning for this current season in our nation, and I am compelled by the Holy Spirit to speak out. This message was given me specifically for my White Evangelical brothers and sisters as related to the treatment of our Brown and Black brothers and sisters as well as the foreigner (immigrant), poor, orphans, widows, and strangers among us.

Jesus said that whatever we do to the least of our brothers is what we are doing to Him (Matthew 25:40). Scripture also tells us that we cannot love God whom we cannot see if we do not love our brothers and sisters—Black, Brown, or any other hue—whom we do see (1 John 4:20). We must all acknowledge the current widespread division within the Evangelical church, a division drawn largely along racial lines. As Christians and members of God's family, we know that this division ought not to be. But there is no agreement as to the specific root of the problem or how to resolve it.

I write this book from a place of love but also from the perspective of a Black sister in Christ. I believe many White Evangelicals are pursuing what they deem to be God's path but have been misinformed, distracted from the truth, and at times politically brainwashed in areas of social justice, our nation's history of race relations, and the situation confronting many minority citizens today. Like the Israelites to whom Ezekiel was called to speak, the church needs a push in the right direction, placing our eyes back on Jesus and not on mankind.

In the following chapters, I will be shining a spotlight on the reality of the African-American community since its arrival on this continent and more specifically, the African-American church. I will also be focusing on what is the reality today for many African-American and other minority citizens of the United States—including an inequitable justice system. And I will be addressing the role the White Evangelical church has played—intentionally or not—in race relations, systemic racism, and continued social injustice in our nation.

Much of the book content comes from a thesis I researched and wrote on this topic for my recently completed Ph.D. in Christian Organizational Leadership. It is written from the perspective that the Bible is the reliable, trustworthy Word of God written by the inspiration of the Holy Spirit. We will be taking a closer look at what Scripture has to say about loving the "other" among us, whether they be of different race, immigrants, poor, orphans, widows, strangers.

In the current racial divide within the Evangelical church, are we following God's will, His Word, and His teachings as outlined in the Holy Scriptures? Only there will we find any lasting solutions to a racially divided nation and/or church. In writing this book, my only objective is to be obedient to the Holy Spirit in blowing the trumpet as one of many faithful watchmen God has placed on the city walls of our nation to deliver His word of truth.

Father God, I pray that through this book the Holy Spirit will speak with conviction and deliverance to the White Evangelical members of Your flock. I pray that they will receive Your servant with the heartfelt love in which these words have been written. That they will acknowledge Truth and become true doers of Your commands in treating all God's children with justice, love, and equality. In the love of Christ and Jesus's matchless precious Name. Amen!

CHAPTER ONE

THE COMING STORM

I 've mentioned that the spiritual gift God has given me is that of prophecy and vision, which sometimes allows me to "see" things that will occur. In biblical terminology, this spiritual gift is termed a Seer. Many of these dreams/visions have been warnings related to a family member, acquaintance, or other individual. Others are personal words from God such as guidance in a career move or healing for a physical condition. When this is the case, the dreams and visions are typically given to me shortly before the prophesied event. I have an entire scrapbook of dreams and visions I've documented in my journal that came to pass.

But when a world event is involved, the Holy Spirit will usually reveal it to me well in advance—sometimes months or even years in advance. As the time comes closer to fulfillment, the frequency of the dreams/visions increases and there is a sense of urgency in my spirit. This occurred before Hurricane Katrina devastated my home city of New Orleans. I had multiple dreams of killer hurricanes, twisters, and great fires destroying the city while I did all possible to warn and rescue my family members, church community, and others.

About three weeks before Hurricane Katrina, I had such a vivid vision of disaster that I called all my family members to warn them that something catastrophic was coming to New Orleans. I urged them to evacuate and offered sanctuary where I was then living in Austin, TX. More and more dreams kept coming closer and closer together

Two days before Katrina hit, I called my brother Rodd and told him that he and his family needed to evacuate immediately. They were in imminent danger. They evacuated the next morning. I began calling my other family members, urging them to join me in my large house in Austin. Most did evacuate, and soon my house was overflowing. That Monday Katrina hit. At first it seemed New Orleans had been spared. Then we received news of the levees bursting. The home of my brother Rodd's mother-in-law, where his family was then living, was struck by a large tree. Many family members now sheltering with me in Austin had lost everything but what they brought with them. But they were alive. My family was safe.

Over the year that followed and beyond until I transitioned to my next career assignment and sold that house, many other dispossessed New Orleans family members came to Austin for comfort and shelter. God provided for them all. The well-paying job, extra car, and big house God had given me were all His provision for His people!

This entire experience reaffirmed to me that God had given me a gift as a Seer. But it also scared me as I didn't want to be the bearer of sad and catastrophic news. How much safer it would be to simply keep silent and hide what God revealed. But if God calls you to be a watchman, you cannot be obedient to God and remain silent. If you do remain silent and the people are not warned, they may reap the results of their own behavior, but the watchman too will be held to account (Ezekiel 33).

Which leads me to the present and why I've told you all the above. About 2013, I began to receive visions of destructive tornados hitting different parts of the United States. In one particular dream, an angel warned me to flee as buildings, roads, and trees began collapsing under the approaching tornado. Snatching up my children, I found myself in a large crowd of refugees all heading the same direction downstream.

Their leader insisted I follow him as that was the way to safety. But it was the opposite direction of where the angel had directed me. Deeply worried for the lives of my children, I was torn between trusting this crowd and going along in the same direction or striking out on our own in the direction the angel indicated.

These dreams continued over the next three years. Then in October 2016, I had another extremely vivid, frightening dream of intruders breaking into our home while my husband tried to protect me and my children. My husband and I along with a pastor friend, Dr. Belinda Smith, who was our intercessory prayer partner, had just completed a period of prayer and fasting. Pastor Belinda received a word from the Holy Spirit that we would be receiving a dream from God that would confirm God's message to me in the prior dream.

Later that night, I dreamed of our family taking refuge in what seemed to be some kind of large storm shelter along with an entire caravan of other people. I could see my extended family, church members, and White Evangelical co-workers as though we were all part of a community sheltering there. Opening the shelter door, I saw outside tornado force winds ripping up and blowing away everything that wasn't firmly attached or had a tight cover, including people I knew in my dream were part of the body of Christ.

The storm was so fierce those in the shelter were telling me not to go out. But I was adamant I was going to snatch those in danger into the shelter. I managed to pull them to safety, where we all stayed protected and safe until the storm passed. Still in the dream, the Holy Spirit spoke to me, telling me this dream was from Him. I asked Him to please give me an interpretation of the dream and let me remember it once I woke up.

The Holy Spirit showed me that a catastrophic storm of events was imminent as judgment from God against the United States. It would come suddenly, and it was our responsibility as His servants to be vigilant and snatch/protect those in our own circle/family/congregation from the coming storm.

Has this storm hit, or is it still approaching? Was the sudden rise of COVID-19 that catastrophic event? The BLM movement? Certainly prior to COVID-19, the American stock market, investment portfolios, and general prosperity were all booming. Just a half-year later, we see America in a major depression with skyrocketing COVID deaths, unemployment, and massive unrest due to new instances of police brutality and social injustice. It definitely seems like judgement from God. Or could an even bigger catastrophic event be on its way?

That has not yet been revealed to me. But I do believe God is telling His church to wake up from our slumber (Romans 13:11; Ephesians 5:14; 1 Thessalonians 5:6) and be vigilant in intercessory prayer (Matthew 26:41; Ephesians 6:18; Colossians 4:2) because it is imperative that we should all be about our heavenly Father's business (Luke 2:49).

Which leads to two key visions God gave me just days before the 2016 elections. My prayer partner, Pastor Belinda, and I were engaged in intercessor prayer, which was our custom. One focus of our intercession was the upcoming election.

That night after our prayer time, I had a dream that I was on a business trip with two White colleagues in some Midwest region that had previously been prosperous but in the dream was now economically depressed due to the departure of manufacturing jobs and big industries. The population appeared to be almost entirely White. In the dream, I was looking to buy a home there due to a new job promotion. But as I searched for a home, the community discovered I was African-American and became so hostile I feared my life. My White colleagues and I were forced to turn off all the lights in the house and hide so we wouldn't be harmed.

When I shared the dream with my husband, my sister Gail, and prayer team, I gave them the message I'd received from the Holy Spirit that we would see a sharp rise in White Supremacy and hate crimes and that there would be riots after the election. Please understand that I had no idea then who would win the election. On the contrary, Hillary Clinton was strongly favored in the polls at that time to be the winner.

This was followed by another dream/vision so intense my husband could audibly hear me speaking in tongues and witnessed the fierce spiritual battle in which I was engaged against a demonic spirit. This demonic spirit was represented by a blonde-haired, blue-eyed woman. In the dream/vision, the Holy Spirit told me that the demonic spirit I was battling was called Aryan.

Upon awakening, I shared this vision with my husband and a cousin who was a former FBI agent and strong supporter of Donald

Trump. I was not familiar with the term Aryan, but a quick internet search indicated a connection with White Supremacy. I discovered that Aryanism is actually a belief propagandized by the Nazis asserting that the Aryan people are superior to all other races and that White Europeans are the descendants of the Aryan race.

I shared my findings with my cousin, who assured me from twenty-five years of firsthand law enforcement knowledge that up to the 2016 election there'd been minimal radical activity related to White Supremacist hate groups in the United States. Sadly, just as the Holy Spirit had revealed, the uptick in White Supremacy has been sharp and growing since the 2016 election, emboldened by Trump's racist rhetoric, close alignment with the "fine people" of the Charlottesville violence, as well as the unwavering White Evangelical support of Trump and refusal to speak out for any accountability of Trump's language, actions, and constant mistruths.

That same week of the 2016 election, I had more dreams regarding the coming storm that included fires burning in major cities across the United States. In one dream, the coming storm was engulfing half the country. I also saw adults and children in cages like concentration camps and war ships massing on our coasts.

Sadly, we've seen all these visions come to pass under Trump's administration. Thousands of immigrant families applying peacefully for asylum have found themselves in concentration camp-like living. Children have been separated from their parents with many still not reunited to this day. This is not how God commanded us to treat the strangers, poor, widows, orphans!

Meanwhile, peaceful protestors against police brutality have been met with batons, tear gas, rubber bullets, and arrest. Which in turn has indeed spawned violence, destruction, looting, and fires as I saw in my visions. Not just in the United States but around the world as people of all races and cultures have taken to the streets to protest how Black people were being treated in the supposed global center of peace, freedom, and justice. With COVID-19 and the stirring up of hate against immigrants, we've also seen an upswing in military mobilization on our borders, including ships, to "protect" against immigrant "others" portrayed as the enemy—or even to keep cruise ships from sneaking passengers ashore!

Ironically, today it is the rest of the world that is restricting the arrival of Americans across their borders as COVID-19 rages in our own country even as it is brought under control elsewhere. Meanwhile there is genuine threat as Russia and other nations make no secret of their continued plans to subvert our elections and politics for their purposes.

Is any or all this the storm I saw? Or is far more to come? Again, it has never been my wish to be bearer of sad and catastrophic events. I wish these warnings were not coming true.

What I do know and what all believers should understand is that the world we live in is going to get worse before Jesus returns. The deception in the land is going to be very strong. The labor pains are intensifying. World powers are flexing their authority. As lawlessness abounds, the hearts of men are going to wax cold (Matthew 24:12). Hatred towards one another is going to increase.

As brothers and sisters in the family of God, whatever our ethnicity or political persuasion, we cannot let ourselves be distracted by these foolish traps. We have to call out the lies and warn the people! As a watchman called to sound the trumpet of alarm, I am making sure that my hands are clean as I obey my heavenly Father.

I pray that you will prayerfully consider what God would have you to do in preparation for these coming storms. Seek His face, asking God to confirm via His Word and through the Holy Spirit's communing with your spirit what specifically is your assignment in this moment of time. Make sure you are on the right side. Not a Democrat side or a Republican side, but God's side doing God's work for God's kingdom. Amen!

CHAPTER TWO

IT'S STILL THERE!

P erhaps one of the biggest enduring myths within White America
and specifically that twenty-five percent of Americans
identifying as White Evangelicals is that racism is a thing of the past.
At best, pre-Civil War. At minimum, pre-Civil Rights Era.

This could not be more wrong, as I and virtually every other
African American can share from personal experience. I remember
vividly one of my earliest encounters with White racism within the
institutional church. It was the late 1960s and I was just six years old
when my sister Lisa and I with four other "Creole" kids attended Camp
Abbey's Christian Summer Camp in Covington, Louisiana. The
remaining two hundred-plus campers were all White children.

Our parents had instilled in Lisa and me and the other Creole
campers that we were all God's children and of equal value with any
other human being. So when our cabin proposed doing a skit about
Cinderella for talent night, I proposed another very pretty Creole girl,
Sandra, to be Cinderella. We were stunned to be abruptly told that as
African Americans we'd already been assigned to be the ugly

stepsisters. We adamantly protested that we deserved lead roles as much as White campers and refused to play our designated roles of "ugly" stepsisters. We also engaged with our White cabinmates, explaining how their treatment made us feel and that racism was wrong.

As a result, the skit was changed into something more inclusive where we could all participate on an equal basis. This was not only my first real memory of racism but also of the encouraging truth that open, honest dialogue and mutual good intentions could change entrenched racist attitudes and behavior.

Some years later while attending a private Christian secondary school, I had experimented with straightening my hair. When I showed up at school with the new "White" hairstyle, my White teacher immediately told me I should always wear my hair like that because it made me pretty. When I reported her comment to my mother, my mother instructed me to tell my teacher that God had created me in His image and I was beautiful regardless of how I wore my hair.

As a Louisiana Creole, my religious heritage was Catholic. I'd purchased a Bible as a teenager while attending a Christian school and occasionally read it. But my faith wasn't personal to me until I accepted Jesus Christ as my Lord and Savior during my first year of college while attending a revival service at a Protestant Evangelical church. Over the following months, God gave me a lasting love for His Word. I spent hours each day reading my Bible and shared my new faith with everyone I met.

That following year was a pivotal point of my life. I spent the entire summer fasting and praying because that's what followers of Jesus did in the Bible. I continued attending the church where I'd been introduced to Jesus and became increasingly involved in youth ministry and street outreach. It was a phenomenal time of experiencing the Holy Spirit's supernatural power, including miracles, signs, wonders, and speaking in tongues. I had the privilege of being used by God to lead hundreds of family and friends to Christ, including my mother. A woman who had struggled with alcohol and immoral relationships, my mother was completely transformed by the Holy Spirit into the epitome of a virtuous woman, and God in turn used her to bring thousands to Himself.

In the summer of 1982, I volunteered to join Dave Wilkerson's youth crusades in Washington, DC. I'd seen the movie about his ministry, *The Cross and the Switchblade*, but didn't know him personally when I joined his team in DC. We were in one of the more crime-infested, poverty-stricken urban projects the first time I heard him address a crowd of thousands. The anointing of the Holy Spirit and Dave's compassion for the lost was palpable as he spoke, and I saw him weep with the heart of God over the lost multitudes of that city. Thousands accepted Christ as Savior during the days of that crusade.

What stood out about Dave Wilkerson was how he partnered with local pastors—most of them Black, some Hispanic—to reach the lost and disciple new Christians. It was at this time that Dave Wilkerson became my spiritual mentor, not because of his fame but his love for God, love for the lost, spiritual discipline in fasting and praying, and his commitment to please God rather than man. I became a financial partner to his ministry. After he founded Time Square Church in New York City, I was privileged to attend there when my job took me to NYC. Attending TSC was like a glimpse of heaven with members from tribes and nations and ethnicities and skin colors all over the planet.

When I later married my husband, Dr. Rev. Gaylord Neal, I discovered he too had been greatly impacted by Dave Wilkerson's ministry. In fact, his son, my stepson, graduated from a Wilkerson-founded school of ministry and served an internship with Pastor Colon Carter, who succeeded Dave Wilkerson as senior pastor of Time Square Church. Throughout my life and even in his death, Dave Wilkerson continues to influence my life and the life of my family, and I still cherish photos I have of my mother, myself, and friends dining with Dave and his wife Gwen.

What a contrast to my experiences attending a predominantly White Evangelical church in New Orleans and in outreach ministry. I was one of about forty college youth from our church who traveled to DC to participate in the David Wilkinson youth crusades. A White suburban church hosted our team. Four of us single young women were assigned to sleeping quarters that consisted of a queen-size sofa bed and a chair, including another Black young woman, Susan, and two White members of our megachurch's worship team.

The two White young women immediately informed Susan and me that we would need to sleep on the floor while they shared the bed. When Susan and I confronted the young women about their assumption, they began arguing, "We're not racist! At least not like our parents and grandparents."

Susan and I tried to explain that the very fact that they felt entitled to the best accommodations based on their race gave clear evidence of their racism. We ended up dialoguing for hours, which included many tears as well as honest, candid, intense moments of fellowship. In the end, our two White roommates admitted wrong-doing and apologized. But once we returned to our home church in Louisiana, they never interacted with Susan and me again.

During my family's time at this church, a prominent White church member, Phyllis, had been assigned to my mother's home Bible study since she lived in our geographical area. She asked church leadership to put her in a White group as she'd feel more comfortable. But the church leader in charge told her that our home was the only Bible study group in her area and admonished her to attend. A widow, my mother had the gift of hospitality and graciously welcomed Phyllis and other White Evangelical women into her home Bible study. She also tangibly demonstrated the true love of Jesus Christ to them by turning the other cheek, visiting them when they were sick, providing food, comforting, and continuously ministering through the Holy Spirit.

After attending our Bible study for a while, Phyllis invited her sister Carol and a White friend, Audrey, co-owner of a national glass company. A vocal White Supremist, Audrey's husband forbade her to fraternize with Blacks, but she would sneak over to my mother's house to fellowship and participate in the Bible study. Eventually, Audrey and Carol accepted Jesus as Lord and Savior.

Decades later at my mother's memorial service, Phyllis described my mother as her best friend and gave public testimony of how she'd been transformed from a White racist through knowing my mother. All three women testified that before meeting my mother and family, they'd believed White people were superior and admitted their prejudices that Blacks were lazy, incapable, and to be feared. They'd resented Affirmative Action and felt society was making too much of racism. The very thought of participating in any personal gathering with Blacks, much less staying in the same living quarters, horrified them, and they admitted the many times they'd witnessed and even in participated in overt acts of racial discrimination. Other White women who'd been part of my mother's home Bible study circle gave similar testimonies at her memorial.

Meanwhile, my oldest sister Debbie had graduated from a Christian high school that was 99% White with just three Blacks in her graduating class. A classmate from one of New Orleans' wealthiest families apologized to Debbie just before graduation that her father wouldn't permit her to invite Debbie to her upscale graduation party because her family was White Supremist.

Later Debbie became a Sunday school teacher at her largely White Evangelical church in Georgia. One six-year-old pupil called her a "nigger" when she warned him that he'd be sent to sit with his parents in the main service if he didn't behave.

"That's a very hateful word," she responded gently. "You should be happy to be in my class so you can learn to love Black people because I was created in God's image too. The Bible says you can't love God, who you can't see, if you don't love your brothers and sisters who you can see. So if you want to love God and go to heaven, you need to love Black people too."

By this point, I'd finished my college degree focused on business finance and corporate leadership. At twenty-four years old, I was promoted as the Western Regional Accounting Branch Manager and assigned to Salt Lake City, which has a Black population of less than one percent. I immediately sought out an Evangelical church of the denomination I had attended in New Orleans. When I seated myself in a pew near the center of the church, every eye turned my direction. Those already seated in that pew immediately stood up and moved to another location.

Later in my career, I worked as Vice President of Finance for a company in North Carolina. The church I attended was again largely White Evangelical, and we were taught from the pulpit that being a God-fearing Evangelical required voting Republican. I voted for and supported many Republican candidates like Ronald Reagan. But when George W. Bush ran for president, I could not support him.

Among other issues, my research indicated that he lived in and/or supported "White's only" neighborhoods and clubs. As a Black person, how could I support someone who would not live around Black people like me? I tried to explain to my White brothers and sisters in the church that this went against everything I knew about Christ. But they could not understand my feelings or how as a Christian I could refuse to vote for a Republican.

God has gifted me in finance and corporate leadership, so throughout my professional career, I've typically been the highest-ranking "minority" within both secular and Christian companies I've worked for. I've also been told routinely, as though it were some kind of compliment, that my hard work and success made me an "exception" for Black people or "not really Black." I was told by one boss, whom I'd deeply respected to that point, that my only other Black colleague, a highly educated, skilled, beautiful woman, was too dark of hue to be considered for promotion.

My family and I currently live in Delaware, where my husband Gaylord is the senior pastor of a technology-based "church without walls" called *A Higher Dimension Church*, which we co-founded in 2013 and now has members in eight states and two countries. While continuing to work in finance, I also serve with Gaylord in pastoral ministry and recently received my Ph.D. in Christian Organizational Leadership. We have twin daughters, who are now ten years old, and four older stepchildren, including a twenty-seven-year-old stepson serving in full-time ministry, as well as five grandchildren.

We live in a fairly affluent majority-White neighborhood. Sadly, I've had to explain to a grandson who was living with us at the time that he can't wear a hoody at night or walk alone from our neighbor's house after dark. We had to explain to him as well as our young daughters how to act when, not if, they are stopped by police and how they as Blacks cannot expect the same treatment as Whites, in and out of the church.

Last school year, my twins were sent a horrifically graphic video from another student at their elementary school featuring a clip from a rap song with someone pretending to shoot them and chanting, "Shoot the niggers, one dead, two dead, now four dead," etc. My girls responded with another video that simply told the sender she wasn't being a true friend to send such unkind material.

I was shocked when the school principal and counselor called my girls in without my presence to tell them their actions weren't becoming of good girls. When I showed the principal the video my daughters had received, she dismissed it with the comment, "Well, that's how kids talk now and the type of music they listen to!"

So two Black girls telling a White girl that sending a vile video is not being a good friend merits administrative intervention and discipline. But a White girl sending an explicit video pretending to shoot Black students is just exercising freedom of speech! It wasn't until I escalated the matter to the school district that the White sender of the original video received any consequences at all.

Meanwhile political bullying within the church remains a problem. One of my daughters-in-law is active in youth leadership of a large multi-cultural church in New York City. Not long ago, she was pulled aside by a spiritual leader and told she'd be blackballed from leadership if she continued expressing concerns regarding Trump and racism. She is far from alone in being pressured to support Trump as a litmus test of fitness for church leadership. In fact, White Evangelical leaders like Franklin Graham, Jerry Falwell, Paula White, and others have called any opposition to Trump demonic and questioned the salvation of anyone who doesn't support him.

Meanwhile, Trump has blatantly expressed his association with the "fine men and women" of White Supremist groups. He has called African American nations of origin "shit-holed nations." He has embraced Confederate rhetoric and made perfectly clear in his actions, deeds, and policies how he feels about non-Whites of any stripe and color. Yet Black Evangelicals are being told we must embrace him, and our very faith as Christians is being questioned if we don't vote for him.

Do you not see our hurt here? Do you not see the hypocrisy? Do you not care about our pain?

In summary, I have been a Black Evangelical for more than thirty years now. I have experienced overt and covert racism in and out of the church as has my family. I have also experienced individual kindness, love, and mentoring from White Evangelical friends, church members, and colleagues. Neither I nor my immediate family have suffered racism to the extent of being arrested for "driving Black," refused promotion for having too dark a skin hue as my colleague above, barred from "Whites only" neighborhoods, much less unjust death like George Floyd, Breonna Taylor, Tamir Rice, or Walter Scott.

So why am I speaking out now? In part, precisely because I've known many loving, kind, God-fearing White Evangelicals who would be appalled to be called racist. Who in their individual interactions with minorities pride themselves on treating them as equals. Who would be the first to denounce the White Supremist behavior described above. All without ever confronting whether systemic racism or racialization (i.e., the processes by which social structures and institutional systems such as housing, employment, and education are defined by race vs. other social characteristics) continue to exist on a corporate level within the spheres of their own churches, communities, and social networks.

My personal experience as well as that of every research survey done over the past generation reveals clearly that White Evangelicals who connect their understanding of biblical Christianity with an equally biblical charge of becoming a more holistic, racially diverse community that addresses social ills and injustices as well as theological and moral issues are by far the minority. This disconnect from corporate social responsibility is at the heart of racialization, as we will discuss more fully later. That is, the individual Christian can be moral and good while demonstrating little if any awareness of their larger group's participation in and contribution to oppressive and/or unjust socio-political systems.

There was a time when White Evangelicals were at the forefront of speaking out against slavery, child labor, appalling work and social conditions, cruel and unusual punishment, and more. Even then, this was largely on an individual basis rather than by support of the White Christian establishment of their time, which more often than not opposed and even punished or jailed those who spoke out. Where now are the White Evangelicals speaking out on continued systemic racism, police brutality, and such horrific acts of violence as perpetrated against George Floyd, Breonna Taylor, Tamir Rice, Walter Scott, and countless other Blacks and other minorities?

Many White Evangelicals may honestly claim ignorance. More so, they are not aware of the historical context of what their Black brothers and sisters have endured, not just during slavery but since. They don't know what the Jim Crow laws were or how "Black codes" returned many freed slaves to involuntary servitude. They have no idea the extent of how Blacks were denied the right to vote, good jobs, education, decent housing, fair policing, and the fundamentals on which Whites built the American dream so that the median net assets of a Black family remain a fraction of a White family from the same social and economic demographic.

Because of this, they don't understand why Black brothers and sisters are angered at a denial of White Privilege. They don't understand why protestors march when a Black person is gunned down by law enforcement. Not just in anger but in fear that their own sons and daughters could be next for the crime of being in the wrong place at the wrong time with the wrong hue of skin. They don't understand why there is such moral outrage when Trump defends White Supremists or dismisses entire demographics of American citizens as inferior, stupid, lazy, violent, and prone to crime. When the socially and economically deprived are blamed as "losers" rather than conceding the smallest contributory responsibility from those who built their own wealth off the oppressed.

It is my hope that reading these chapters will dispel ignorance and open eyes as to the heartfelt point of view of your Black brothers and sisters in God's family. But also that they will soften hearts and create a bridge of understanding that truly brings God's people together as "neither Jew nor Gentile, neither slave nor free, nor is there male and female, for you are all one in Christ Jesus" (Galatians 3:28) for "he himself [Christ] is our peace, who has made the two groups one and has destroyed the barrier, the dividing wall of hostility . . . to reconcile both of them to God through the cross" (Ephesians 2:14-16; see also Colossians 3:11).

CHAPTER THREE

HOW DID WE GET HERE?

Efforts over the past fifty years to build racial bridges between the White Evangelical church and their Black brothers and sisters are fighting against centuries of church-sanctioned racism and racial rationalization. Martin Luther King and former Episcopal Bishop James A. Pike of New York are two major religious leaders who have famously stated: "The eleven o'clock hour on Sunday is the most segregated hour in American life."

Sadly, that remains the case in much of the United States, above all within the Evangelical movement. To understand why this has been so difficult, we must go back to the beginning and examine some of Black American history that is too seldom taught in schools, especially in White majority classrooms.

Neither slavery nor racism began with White Christianity. Both have been around for all of documented human history when virtually any other people group, conquered nations, and the poorer classes of one's own race were routinely sold into slavery and considered inferior and less than human.

But it was within White Christian Europe, reaching prominence during the fifteenth and sixteenth centuries, that an obsession rose with how the origins and/or causes of dark skin could be reconciled with the biblical narrative that every human is a descendent of the original parents, Adam and Eve. Rooted in notions of White Europeans being God's chosen people and having been given dominion over creation, European church-states initiated the creation of racialization based on skin color and purity/goodness.

The reason was simple and even logical. How did cultures converted largely to Christianity whose leadership claimed to follow the teachings of Scripture and the example of Jesus Christ justify the continued oppression and enslaving of other human beings? As enslaving fellow White Christians of any nationality became less and less acceptable, the misquoted and taken out of context Noahic "curse" on the "Sons of Ham" (Genesis 9:25-27) was dug up and dusted off.

The actual Genesis passage speaks of Ham's son Canaan being subjugated by some of Shem's future descendants, the people of Israel. This prophecy came true when God led Israel from Egypt to conquer the land of Canaan, dispossessing its depraved, evil population (Exodus). No historical evidence supported any particular correlation of Shem and Ham with White and Black races. In fact, Scripture itself identifies two prominent African cultures, Sheba and Ophir, as descendants of Shem while descendants of Ham included the Babylonian and Assyrian empires as well as today's Middle East and future Israel (see Genesis 10).

But such inconvenient data was ignored as fifteenth and sixteenth century White church leaders eagerly identified the Black and Brown races as the "Sons of Ham" and White Europeans as the "Sons of Shem," thereby justifying the subjugation of the "Sons of Ham" by "Sons of Shem" as preordained by God Himself. Blacks and Browns were not only condemned by God to be in perpetual servitude to Whites. They were also intellectually inferior and more sinful, depraved, and prone to violence. I.e., "the darker the skin, the darker the sin."

A biblical "injunction" for White Christians to subjugate Black and Brown races became justification for the slave trade and for building White Christian colonial empires across "heathen" Africa, Asia, and the Native people groups of the Americas and Oceana. Travel writings from this period reinforced the European self-understanding that they were the children of God and children of light while non-White Europeans were by definition "outside of the light."

WHITE EVANGELISM AND SLAVERY

By the time of the Great Awakening in the early eighteenth century, the beginning of Evangelicalism and Christian revival across the American colonies, most American White Christians did not consider African Americans fully human and therefore did not believe African Americans had souls. This again justified treating them like any other beast of burden, including breeding them as one would breed cattle for personal property and sale and forbidding any normal human marriage and family life. It would be impossible to describe the level of pain and suffering inflicted as children were ripped away from parents to be sold like one more litter of pigs or puppies.

Even when views changed as to the basic humanity of Blacks, Native Americans, and other non-White races, religious leaders continued to justify slavery by teaching that slave traders and owners were fulfilling their Christian duty in enslaving Africans. Since Africans were of an inferior nature incapable of ruling, guiding, or controlling themselves, slavery actually offered them the opportunity of conversion to Christianity, thereby giving them useful purpose in this life as obedient, humble servants to Whites and the hope of heaven in the next life. When the United States became a nation, its new Constitution enshrined the inferior status of Black Americans by defining their value as three-fifths that of a White American.

Ironically, even as many slaves did convert to Christianity, many White Evangelical slave owners resisted their conversion for fear that learning biblical teachings like brotherhood and oneness in Christ would lead to slave revolts. In consequence, White Evangelical church leaders who were also slave owners, such as George Whitfield, Charles Finny, Cotton Mather and others, not only taught biblical support of slavery but that any necessary means of punishment was justified against slaves who rebelled against their White Christian masters. Emphasis in converting slaves was on them becoming humble, obedient, honest, hardworking servants to their masters and being grateful for the opportunity to exchange their heathen heritage for Christian servitude and eventual eternal life.

By the 1830s, many northern White Evangelicals had come to believe that slavery went against the ideals they'd fought for in the American Revolutionary War and became outspoken abolitionists. But in speaking out against slavery, they did not go so far as to speak out against racism. Most believed interracial relationships were un-Christian and held deep fears of "miscegenation." Church leaders also still typically called for segregated congregations and resisted instilling Black people into church leadership or as elders.

In the South, White Evangelical church leaders systematically used the Bible and church doctrine to defend slavery. Beyond such arguments as biblical figures owning slaves and the so-called "charitable altruisms" that slavery facilitated African Americans becoming Christians, a strong justification of White Evangelicals was the idea that Christians should focus on evangelism, stay out of politics, and not seek to make any changes to existing laws.

RECONSTRUCTION ERA

In January 1865, an amendment to the Constitution to abolish slavery in the United States was proposed by Congress. Almost a year later on December 18, 1865, it was ratified as the Thirteenth Amendment, formally abolishing slavery throughout the United States of America. During the initial Reconstruction period of 1865 to 1877, federal laws provided civil rights protections in the American South for freedmen, i.e., African Americans who had formerly been slaves, as well as for a small minority of Blacks who had been free before the Civil War.

During this short window of time, great changes came to the South. Black schools were started. Blacks were participating in politics, being appointed to boards of education, judgeships, military leadership. Black churches were built. Northern churches, charitable agencies, and mission organizations sent aid, missionaries, and educators.

Life certainly wasn't easy for four million African-American former slaves suddenly left without employment, education, homes, or even the most basic of personal possessions. It has been estimated that up to a million liberated slaves, or almost a quarter of the southern African-American population, died of starvation, disease, and exposure within the decade following Emancipation. But there was an air of optimism and determination to build a better, freer world for the next generation.

So what happened?

In essence, the Civil War technically ended slavery, but it could not change human hearts. Far from racial reconciliation in or out of the church, defeated White southerners for the most part deeply resented, feared, and, yes, hated the newly-free Black population. In the beginning, federal oversight and even Union troops stationed in the south guaranteed basic citizenship rights of southern Blacks. But as government was returned to state control, the dominant White population rapidly took back control of local government and made it their mission to keep Blacks "in their place."

Politically, this mean White Democrats regaining power over Republican opponents throughout the south. Please understand here that where these two political parties stood then have nothing to do with twenty-first-century party platforms of these two parties. It is ironic that White Evangelical supporters of Trump today will congratulate themselves as the party that ended slavery when their positions and attitudes toward non-Whites are far more in tune with the southern White Democrats of post-Civil War Reconstruction.

White Democrats used insurgent paramilitary groups such as the White League and the Red Shirts to disrupt Republican organizing, run Republican officeholders out of town, and intimidate Black people to suppress their voting. Extensive voter fraud was also used. In one instance, an outright coup insurrection in coastal North Carolina led to the violent removal of democratically elected non-Democrat party executive and representative officials, who were then hunted down or hounded out. Gubernatorial elections in my own state of Louisiana were close and had been disputed for years. But 1868 onward saw increasing violence against Black voters during campaigns.

Within a decade, the initial optimism that freedom would offer the African-American community the same opportunities to pursue the American dream as their White neighbors quickly dissipated as many of the social injustices of slavery were simply perpetrated under another name. Sadly, war-weary northerners who had spoken out and even fought for abolition of slavery had by now for the most part abandoned any interest in jeopardizing their own political and social interests by pursuing lasting social reform in the South. As freed slaves began moving north in search of work, threatening a White monopoly on jobs within the booming industrial revolution, White attitudes toward the influx of African Americans began to mirror their southern neighbors.

Then in 1877 came what to the Black community seemed a total betrayal of the very principles on which the United States claimed to be founded. Major allegations of corruption, massive Black voter suppression in swing states, and a highly contested presidential election created a gridlock in the Electoral College that left Congress stepping in to choose a winner. In what has been called the Compromise of 1877, a bargain corrupt by any measure, Democrats agreed to accept the Republican presidential nominee, Rutherford Hayes, on the condition that all remaining federal troops be withdrawn from the South.

With a stroke of a signatory pen, White Democrats regained political power in every Southern state, and the minimal protection offered by federal military presence was stripped from the Black community. It would be impossible in these pages to scratch the surface of social injustice that resulted. But a few examples will give a glimpse into what remains painful historical memory for today's African-American community.

BLACK CODES

The Thirteenth Amendment to the Constitution, ratified in 1865, states: "Neither slavery nor involuntary servitude, ***except as a punishment for crime*** whereof the party shall have been duly convicted, shall exist within the United States, or any place subject to their jurisdiction."

Did you catch that exemption to slavery? This clause is precisely what is applied today to require convicted prisoners in state and federal prisons to carry out work in exchange for costs of incarceration. But in the Reconstruction Era south, it became a weapon to return Blacks to servitude. The overwhelming majority of White Southern farmers and business owners were furious when the Thirteenth Amendment took away slave labor. To appease them, the federal government turned a blind eye when in 1866, just one year after the Thirteenth Amendment was ratified, southern states including Alabama, Texas, Louisiana, Arkansas, Georgia, Mississippi, Florida, Tennessee, and South Carolina used this clause to establish laws called Black Codes.

Blacks found guilty of violating these codes were imprisoned, then leased out to the same businesses that had lost slaves through the passage of the Thirteenth Amendment, a system of convict labor known as peonage. Men, women, and children were rounded up and transported to plantations where they would harvest cotton, tobacco, sugar cane, and other crops. Or they would be leased to work at coal mines or railroad companies. The owners of these businesses would pay the state for every prisoner who worked for them.

Among such Black Codes was the "sundown law," a policy in many towns and cities that made it illegal for Blacks to be out after dark. Versions of sundown laws remained on the books well into the twentieth century with some reported arrests on such charges taking place as recently as 1998. Likewise, if a Black could not prove they had a job, they could be arrested on the spot on the charge of vagrancy or loitering. Realistically, this meant a Black needed a White employer to vouch for them that they were gainfully employed.

Even worse, if the parent of a Black child was categorized as a "vagrant," the judicial system allowed the police and/or other government agencies to seize their children as well to be "apprenticed" to an "employer." Males could be held until the age of twenty-one while females could be held until they were eighteen. Their "employers" had the legal right to inflict punishment on the child for any perceived disobedience and to recapture them if they ran away. In other words, while their parents were sent off to unpaid involuntary servitude through the prison system, the children were placed directly into unpaid involuntary servitude until they reached adulthood. Slavery by another name is still slavery!

A more extreme example of Black Codes in Louisiana made it illegal for a Black man to preach to Black congregations without special permission in writing from the chief of police. If caught, he could be arrested and fined. If he could not pay the fines, which were unbelievably high, he would be sentenced to servitude until his debt was paid off. This became a way for southern Whites to exercise control over Black churches even after emancipation.

All of this made the business of arresting Blacks very lucrative, not just for businesses and plantation owners but for the state governments. Which is why hundreds of White men were hired by these states as police officers. It is estimated that almost a million African-American men, women, and children ended up becoming part of the system of peonage, or re-enslavement through the prison system. Nor was this for just a short time period. State sanctioned and imposed peonage across the south didn't end until after the beginning of World War II around 1940.

Like slavery itself, this system of peonage is an example of systemic racism. That is, racism established and perpetuated by government systems. Slavery was made legal by the United States government. Black Codes, peonage, and the later Jim Crow laws and enforced segregation were all made legal by the United States government and upheld by the judicial system. These acts of racism were built into the system, which is where the term "systemic racism" is derived.

CHAPTER FOUR

JIM CROW

T he Compromise of 1877 marked the formal end of Reconstruction. With any federal oversight removed from defeated Confederate states, state legislatures across the South now had the political power to roll back virtually all political and economic gains made by the Black community during the Reconstruction period. A series of state and local laws were enacted that disenfranchised Black citizens and enforced racial segregation in the Southern United States. Incredibly, most of these laws would not be repealed until the Civil Rights era almost a century later.

These laws became known as Jim Crow laws. Why this name? The origin was actually a song-and-dance routine by White actor Thomas Rice, considered the father of Blackface minstrelsy. This form of entertainment, highly popular in the nineteenth century, involved White actors blackening their faces with burnt cork and dressing in rags to satirize their perception of Blacks as lazy, ignorant, and incapable of intelligible speech. Jim Crow was the name Rice gave to the Black slave he portrayed in his act. By the Civil War, "Jim Crow" and "nigger" were both popular pejoratives in referencing Blacks.

In other words, Jim Crow was not a name Blacks gave themselves but one inflicted on them to mock and demean. Which should make clear why dressing up in "Blackface," as certain politicians and leaders of state have been called out for in recent decades, remains so offensive to Black Americans. It also describes precisely how demeaning and repressive these laws were intended to be with the deliberate intent to make Blacks second-class citizens.

In practice, Jim Crow laws mandated racial segregation in all public facilities across the former Confederate States of America and in some other states as well. Disgracefully, Jim Crow laws were actually upheld by the Supreme Court in the 1896 case of *Plessy vs. Ferguson*, which laid out its "separate but equal" legal doctrine for African Americans, a decision now considered to be one of the worst and most unjust a sitting Supreme Court has upheld. The legal doctrine of "separate but equal" argued that separating races did not violate the Constitution or amount to discrimination so long as equal facilities were provided both races.

As with South African apartheid, "separate but equal" was of course an oxymoron from the beginning since "equal" facilities" never existed and any community or state provided facilities for African Americans were consistently inferior and underfunded. Public education had been segregated from the beginning. With Jim Crow laws, all public facilities were segregated, including trains, buses, drinking fountains, restrooms, restaurants, etc. In many places Black facilities didn't exist at all, so a Black person might have no access at all to a public restroom or drinking fountain because the only ones available were for Whites.

Voter Suppression

Jim Crow laws were not just passed to keep races apart but with a far more urgent goal to keep Blacks from impacting the status quo of White dominance through exercising their right to vote. A combination of literacy and comprehension tests, property ownership, and poll taxes made it more and more difficult for Blacks to vote. Especially since the Black community in these decades had minimal access to education so was largely illiterate or semi-literate. Tests were specifically designed to be too difficult for the undereducated to pass. Anyone who had been in prison also lost voting rights, another motive for rounding up Blacks on the flimsiest excuse for the peonage system.

The same laws could also disenfranchise poor illiterate Whites, but a "grandfather" clause permitted an exception if parents or grandparents had voted before 1867 (i.e., end of Civil War). Since this applied to virtually all Whites while Blacks of course had no vote before 1867, the "grandfather" clause simply meant that Whites of the same social demographic as Blacks could vote, but Blacks couldn't. In many places, Whites were exempted altogether from having to take literacy tests.

Nor was voting suppression limited to Jim Crow laws. Blacks who did pass the voting requirements frequently faced violence intended to intimidate "uppity" Blacks from voting. This included not only beatings and lynchings, but burning homes, loss of jobs, and seizure of property. Blacks were not permitted to join a political party, as these were considered private institutions, so only White candidates could run in primaries, meaning that Blacks couldn't run for either state or federal office. White voting officials routinely purged voter rolls of Black voters, so that when Blacks did try to vote, they were told they weren't registered.

As a result of such measures, Black voter turnout dropped drastically throughout the South. In my home state of Louisiana, Black registered voters had been reduced to just over five thousand though they comprised the majority of the state's population. By 1910, only 730 Blacks were registered, less than 0.5% of eligible Black men. In North Carolina Black voters had been completely eliminated from voter rolls by the early 1900s. Similar statistics could be given for any southern state.

Those who couldn't vote were also not eligible to serve on juries or run for local offices, so Black Southerners effectively disappeared from political life even in regions where they were a majority. Since they could not influence the state legislatures, their interests were overlooked, while minority Whites could and did enact laws to continue their own dominance. Even worse, barring Blacks from sitting on juries meant that any legal or criminal case against a Black would be tried by all-White juries. These jury members already blamed Blacks for a Confederate defeat and were predisposed to rule against any Black, whether as defendant or accuser.

Is there any wonder Blacks did not dare report to law enforcement violence, rape, or other injustice perpetrated by Whites? Meanwhile, a Black accused by a White of the smallest offense, such as smiling at a White woman or daring to argue with a White man, could end up in prison or lynched.

One of the most infamous such cases was fourteen-year-old Emmett Till, who in 1955 was accused of whistling at and flirting with a White woman in Mississippi. From Chicago, Till was likely ignorant of local strictures on any interaction at all with White women. But the White woman later admitted that she'd fabricated most of the incident. The woman's husband and brother abducted Till, torturing and mutilating him before killing him. After being found not guilty by an all-White jury, they actually boasted of having carried out the murder.

"Equal" Facilities

Post-Civil War, there was a great thirst for education among African-Americans, both children and adult. The original Reconstruction legislatures as well as aid organizations from the North funded public schools in most Southern states for both Blacks and Whites. There was strong hostility against educating Blacks among Southern Whites, who felt that educated Blacks would not only compete for good jobs but could then vote and enter politics, thereby threatening White political control. As at the voting booth, White Supremists resorted to violence, burning schools, terrorizing both teachers and students to intimidate them from attending school.

Once Jim Crow laws established strict segregation, Black schools were consistently underfunded compared to schools for White children. Public libraries for Black people did not exist at all until the early 1900s and were typically stocked with secondhand books and minimal educational resources. All of which contributed to keeping a good portion of the Black community too poorly educated to pass the rigorous voting registration tests.

The Jim Crow laws, lack of job opportunities, and high rate of lynching as well as other oppressive, unjust policing in the South were major factors that led to the Great Migration of African Americans during the first half of the twentieth century to Northeastern, Midwestern, and Western states in search of better lives. But while the separation of African Americans from the White general population was not as legalized and formalized outside the South, a segregated culture had become common, whether in housing, sports, recreation, or other public activities.

This included professional athletics. White opposition led to the exclusion of African-American athletes from most organized sporting competitions during the Jim Crow period. In baseball, a color bar instituted in the 1880s led to the development of the Negro Leagues, which featured many fine players. A major breakthrough occurred in 1947 when Jackie Robinson was hired as the first African American to play in Major League baseball. Baseball teams continued to integrate in the succeeding years, leading to the full participation of Black baseball players in the Major Leagues by the 1960s.

Blacks were allowed into professional boxing much earlier. African-American boxer Jack Johnson became the first World Colored Heavyweight in 1903 and World Heavyweight Champion in 1908, while Joe Louis held the World Heavyweight title for twelve years from 1937-1949. Joe Gans, rated as the greatest Lightweight boxer of all time, held the World Lightweight title from 1902–1908. Black athletes were also competing in track and field, including athlete Jesse Owens, famed for winning four gold medals at the 1936 Summer Olympics in Berlin, much to the anger of Hitler and other Nazi White Supremists.

Despite the hardship and racial prejudice of the Jim Crow era, several Black entertainers and literary figures also gained broad popularity with White audiences in the early twentieth century, including such luminaries as tap dancers Bill "Bojangles" Robinson and the Nicholas Brothers, jazz musicians Louis Armstrong, Duke Ellington, and Count Basie, and actress Hattie McDaniel, the first Black person to receive an Academy Award as Mammy in *Gone with the Wind*.

Ku Klux Klan

But Jim Crow laws and policies were only part of the forces arrayed against Blacks. They also faced the unofficial policies and practices enforced by the Ku Klux Klan (also known as the KKK and the Klan), a racist, anti-Catholic, anti-Jewish, and anti-immigrant White Supremist organization that claimed to "support law enforcement and traditional morality." Founded during Reconstruction, the Ku Klux Klan quickly mobilized as a vigilante group to intimidate Southern Blacks—and any Whites who would help them—and to prevent them from exercising basic civil rights such as voting or education. Lynching, tar-and-feathering, rape, and other violent attacks on those challenging White Supremacy became KKK hallmarks.

The KKK reached its height of power and influence from the late-nineteenth century to the mid-twentieth century. Historian Leonard Moore documented that during the 1920s between one-quarter and one-third of all native-born White male Americans paid the ten-dollar membership fee to become Klansmen. In some communities, the figure was as high as forty to fifty percent. In many Southern states, the KKK was the largest organization of any kind, and its influence on politics and laws was unparalleled by any other political group. Outlandish titles like Imperial Wizard and Exalted Cyclops, hooded costumes, violent "night rides," and the notion that the group comprised an "invisible empire" conferred a mystique that only added to the Klan's popularity.

After a short but violent initial period, the Klan largely disbanded once Jim Crow laws secured the domination of Southern Whites. In the 1920s, the Klan enjoyed a huge revival, this time directed against immigration, especially Catholic and Jewish. A series of sex scandals, internal power struggles, and newspaper exposés drastically reduced its influence. The Klan arose a third time during the 1960s to oppose the Civil Rights Movement and to preserve segregation in the face of unfavorable court rulings. The Klan's bombings, murders, and other attacks took a great many lives, including four young girls killed while preparing for Sunday services at the 16th Street Baptist Church in Birmingham, Alabama.

According to their propaganda, KKK members as well as adherents of Christian Identity, another White Supremist extreme right-wing religious ideology, believe that the Bible is the family history of the White race. In their ideology, Whites are morally and spiritually superior to other races and the only race that has continuously followed Jesus Christ. They also teach that the Old Testament's Twelve Tribes of Israel represent the origins of the White race (e.g., Anglo-Saxons, Teutonic, Scandinavian, Celtic, Basque, Lombard, Slavic, etc.) and that God created other races as "mud people" with beast-like roles and lower standing to Whites. They condemn race-mixing and Jews, whom they perceive as enemies to God. Such religious interpretation not only de-humanizes non-Whites but provides spiritual justification—and perhaps motivation—to attack non-Whites perceived enemies.

Sadly, the KKK has misappropriated a lot of biblical symbolism for their twisted ideology. For instance, one of their most iconic marks, a burning cross, is equated to sending out the light of Christ to the world. Their white robes and hoods supposedly symbolize purity and righteousness as white linen does in Scripture (Revelation 19:8). Their primary symbol, a white cross with a red blood-drop at the center, is identified as symbolizing the atonement and sacrifice of Jesus Christ on the cross as well as others who have shed their blood for the White race.

Some KKK leaders are actually ordained ministers, and some have even organized churches that enjoy tax-exempt status. Examples include the Church of the National Knights of the KKK, Christian American Knights of the KKK, Knights of the White Disciples, and the Soldiers of the Cross Training Institute.

As I saw in my vision just before the election, there has been a major resurgence of the KKK and other White Supremacy groups since the Trump administration took office.

WOODROW WILSON

As a body of law, Jim Crow institutionalized economic, educational, social, and legal disadvantages for African Americans living in the South. But such laws didn't impact just the South. The United States military was already segregated, and it was Woodrow Wilson, a Southern Democrat, who initiated the segregation of federal workplaces after winning the 1912 presidential election, despite much protest from African-American leaders and White progressive groups in the North and Midwest.

In the Jim Crow context, the 1912 presidential election was already steeply slanted against the interests of Black Americans, since most Black people still lived in the South, where they had been effectively disfranchised. Though a Democrat elected from New Jersey, Woodrow Wilson was born and raised in the South and was the first Southern-born president of the post-Civil War period. Washington, DC, and other federal facilities had been integrated since the end of the Civil War.

But once Wilson began appointing Southerners to his Cabinet, they in turn began pressing for segregated workplaces. One Wilson appointee, Secretary of the Treasury William Gibbs McAdoo, was heard to express his opinion of Black and White women working together in the same office:

> I feel sure that this must go against the grain of the White women. Is there any reason why the White women should not have only White women working across from them on the machines?

Ironically, shortly after initiating federal segregation, Woodrow Wilson addressed a large crowd at Gettysburg for a so-called Peace Jubilee on July 4, 1913, the semi-centennial of Abraham Lincoln's powerful declaration on that very spot that "all men are created equal," moralizing:

> How complete the union has become and how dear to all of us. How unquestioned, how benign and majestic, as state after state has been added to this, our great family of free men!

In response to Wilson's address, a *Washington Bee* editorial wondered if the 1913 Gettysburg event was a reunion of those who fought for "the extinction of slavery" or a reunion of those who fought to "perpetuate slavery and who are now employing every artifice and argument known to deceit" to present emancipation as a failed venture.

Historian David W. Blight notes that Wilson's showy Peace Jubilee "was a Jim Crow reunion, and White Supremacy might be said to have been the silent, invisible master of ceremonies."

CHAPTER FIVE

CIVIL RIGHTS ERA

In 1954, the Supreme Court under Chief Justice Earl Warren ruled in the landmark case *Brown v. Board of Education* that the segregation of state-sponsored public schools was unconstitutional. Implementation was rapid in Northern and Western states but was deliberately stopped in the South by a movement called Massive Resistance, sponsored by segregationists who largely controlled the state legislatures.

In 1955 in Montgomery, Alabama, Rosa Parks refused to give up her seat on a city bus to a White man. She wasn't actually the first. In fact, she'd been inspired by fifteen-year-old Claudette Colvin doing the same thing nine months earlier. But Parks' act of civil disobedience became an important catalyst for civil rights protests and actions. Activists built the Montgomery Bus Boycott around it, which lasted more than a year and resulted in desegregation of privately-run buses in that city.

Much more significant in terms of penetrating the psyche of America was the Civil Rights Movement, especially the actions of the

Southern Christian Leadership Conference (SCLC) spearheaded by Martin Luther King, Jr. This largely displaced the older and more moderate National Alliance for the Advancement of Colored People (NAACP) in assuming leadership roles. Dr. King organized massive demonstrations that attracted massive media attention in an era when network television news was an innovative and universally watched phenomenon. SCLC, student activists, and smaller local organizations staged demonstrations across the South.

In the summer of 1963, there were eight-hundred-plus demonstrations in two-hundred-plus southern cities and towns with over a hundred thousand participants and fifteen thousand arrests. Alabama governor George Wallace escalated the crisis by defying court orders to admit the first two Black students to the University of Alabama. President John F. Kennedy responded by ordering Attorney General Robert Kennedy to file federal lawsuits against segregated schools and to deny funds for discriminatory programs. He also sent a comprehensive civil rights bill to Congress.

As unrest mounted, national attention focused on Birmingham, Alabama, where Bull Connor and his police forces arrested almost a thousand young student protesters on one day alone. The next day Connor unleashed billy clubs, police dogs, and high-pressure water hoses to disperse and punish the young demonstrators with a brutality that horrified the nation and tarnished the image of a modernizing progressive urban South. President Kennedy, who had been calling for moderation, threatened to use federal troops to restore order in Birmingham. Against a backdrop of church bombings and assassinations, the Birmingham mayor finally agreed to a compromise that opened the library, golf courses, and other city facilities to both races.

In August 1963, Dr. Martin Luther King launched a massive march on Washington with more than two hundred thousand demonstrators assembling in front of the Lincoln Memorial, the largest political assembly to that point in national history. The Kennedy administration now gave full-fledged support to the Civil Rights Movement, but powerful Southern congressmen blocked any legislation. After Kennedy was assassinated, President Lyndon Johnson called for immediate passage of Kennedy's civil rights legislation.

In January 1964, President Johnson met with civil rights leaders. On January 8 during his first State of the Union address, Johnson asked Congress to "let this session of Congress be known as the session which did more for civil rights than the last hundred sessions combined."

On June 21, civil rights workers Michael Schwerner, Andrew Goodman, and James Chaney disappeared in Neshoba County, Mississippi, where they were volunteering in the registration of African-American voters. Their disappearance captured national attention, even more so once their murdered, mutilated bodies were found about six weeks later along with the bodies of several other missing student activists. Among those eventually charged with the crimes were a local sheriff and several other members of law enforcement as well as the Imperial Wizard of the KKK. It took a federal investigation to bring indictments after Mississippi officials refused to prosecute the murderers.

The ensuing outrage helped President Johnson and civil rights activists build a bi-partisan coalition in Congress that finally managed to break Southern filibusters and pass Kennedy's civil rights bill. On July 2, 1964, Johnson signed the bill into law. The historic Civil Rights Act was the most powerful affirmation of equal rights ever made by

Congress. It guaranteed equal access to public accommodations such as restaurants and places of amusement. It authorized the Justice Department to bring lawsuits to desegregate school facilities. It gave new powers to the Civil Rights Commission and allowed federal funding to be suspended in cases of proven discrimination. It also outlawed racial, religious, and gender discrimination for apartment housing as well as businesses with twenty-five or more employees.

But voter disenfranchisement still remained a major problem across the South. Education and voter registration programs in Southern states had been underway for some time but had achieved only modest success. The murder of the three voting-rights activists in Mississippi in 1964 and the state's refusal to prosecute the murderers along with numerous other acts of violence and terrorism against Black people had gained national attention. Then came the unprovoked attack on March 7, 1965, by county and state troopers on peaceful Alabama protesters crossing the Edmund Pettus Bridge en route from Selma to the state capital of Montgomery. Once again, national outrage gave impetus for President Johnson and a bi-partisan coalition in Congress to push through effective voting rights enforcement legislation.

The Voting Rights Act of 1965 legally ended sanctioned state barriers to voting for all federal, state, and local elections. It also provided for federal oversight and the monitoring of counties with historically low minority voter turnout. Change didn't come overnight. Years of enforcement have been needed to overcome resistance. Additional legal challenges have been made in the courts to ensure the ability of voters to elect candidates of their choice.

BEYOND THE CIVIL RIGHTS MOVEMENT

Many White people, including White Evangelicals, believe that racism ended after the Civil Rights Movement because overt bigotry and hatred are no longer deemed publicly acceptable. In the post-Civil Rights era, it has been politically correct to be "colorblind," i.e., not being overtly discriminatory or using racist speech.

With the ending of institutional state-sponsored segregation, racism became equated in the mind of many Whites with individual prejudice and/or individual acts of discrimination. This allows them to relegate racism to a few ignorant Whites while ignoring the continued existence of institutions and systems of power based in White privilege. Many Whites today sincerely believe that race problems in the United States are due to minority groups being "stuck in the past" or because minority individuals make poor lifestyle choices.

The reality is that White Privilege—that is, unearned social, political, and economic advantages bestowed on an individual solely based on the color of their skin—remains very much a reality and is simple to prove statistically. From the signing of the Civil Rights Act to the present day, the income disparity between Whites and Blacks has remained virtually unchanged with the median income of Blacks being less than two-thirds that of Whites. Unemployment for Blacks is twice that of Whites, and employment for Blacks remains overwhelmingly in lower-paying jobs. From birth, a White person has better access to education, health insurance, health care.

White Privilege can be seen even more starkly in the legal system where the incarceration rate for Blacks is more than five times higher that of Whites. But there are other less visible privileges. Consider the following examples:

- A White person would *never* be murdered by a police officer kneeling on his neck while bystanders pleaded for his life (as in the case of George Floyd).

- It is unlikely a White person would be gunned down and killed just because he was jogging through a neighborhood (as in the case of Ahmaud Arbery).

- It is unlikely a White person would be shot by police while sleeping in their residence (as in the case of Breonna Taylor).

- It is unlikely a White person would be gunned down by police through her own window because a concerned neighbor called for a "wellness check" (as in the case of Atatiana Jefferson).

- It is unlikely an unarmed White person accosted by law enforcement would be shot and killed.

- Whites can choose to be aware of or to ignore their racial heritage.

- Groups of White youth are allowed to gather in public without being harassed by the police.

- When the media and educators talk about American "civilization," White people are always credited with making it happen.

- A White person can turn on the television or open to the front page of the paper and see White people widely and positively represented.

- A White person doesn't wonder if he/she is being stopped by the police because of his or her race.

- Whites can go to the mall or a restaurant without questioning the kind of service they may receive.

In summary, White Privilege is the inevitable outcome of being the dominant racial power group, and it shapes White identity both as individuals and as a group. Most White Americans see themselves first as individuals rather than members of a racial group. Since individualism and meritocracy are core tenets of White American culture, most have been educated to believe that a person earns his or her social status through merit and that every individual has the option to change her or his life.

Conversely, since not all individual Whites receive the same amount of privilege, many don't consider themselves privileged due to their personal life's circumstances. So they reject the concept of White Privilege as something that gives them status. Such beliefs not only demonstrate misconception of how privilege works in our society, but fail to acknowledge the aggregate social, political, and economic advantages Whites have accumulated as a group due to the socio-political and legal systems that have operated in their favor over the last five hundred years.

It is true that to a certain degree people can change their social status by engaging in certain activities such as pursuing a higher education, enlisting in the military, or garnering fame in the athletic or entertainment arena, etc. That said, an individual's socio-political status within the United States is almost exclusively determined by the group (s) with which a person can be identified based on the individual's race, gender, sexual identity, physical ability, and age.

For example, a White, male, able-bodied person is automatically granted a high degree of privilege within current American culture. Conversely, a non-White, female, and/or disabled person will likely be afforded fewer or even no privileges. A comparison that perhaps helps describe what this feels like to those on the opposite side of the White Privilege divide is that of a five-kilometer race. White Americans will have different physical abilities as far as how fast they will run and who will get ahead in the race. But they at least get to line up on the same starting line.

Consider that same race where the starting line for Asian Americans is a quarter-kilometer behind that of Whites, Hispanics a half-kilometer, while the Black starting line is a full kilometer behind White contenders. There may be Black runners whose prowess is so outstanding they will catch up and even pass a certain percentage of White runners. But for many, simply getting as far as the White starting line will leave them worn out, hopelessly behind, and too discouraged to even bother trying to catch up.

CHAPTER SIX

COVERT RACISM

B ut it is not just White Privilege that remains very much a reality. Sheer unadulterated racism continues very much alive. Sometimes it is overt and easy to detect such as when White Pride and Neo-Nazi groups march in a city streets to the cheers of white spectators or when White crowds at a Trump rally chant about American lawmakers of African or Asian descent, "Send them home!"

But there is perhaps even more racism that is not only covert but subconscious. Take the statement of one young white male who commented: "There are two types of Blacks—African Americans and niggers. African Americans are the ones who at least act white."

To this young man, African American wasn't a less offensive way to identify an American of African descent, but a Black person who was somehow more acceptable because of acting "White," whatever that implied. I've already mentioned my former boss, who treated me as superior to my Black colleague because I was light-complexioned enough to be perceived as Hispanic or some other non-Black ethnicity.

Beyond such subtly racist language, there are also subtly racist gestures routinely made by White people when in the company of non-Whites that they might not perceive as racist or even consciously notice but are deeply hurtful and offensive to the Blacks who encounter them on a regular basis. Such gestures include sudden changes in posture or body language when a non-White approaches. Nonverbal behaviors such as hurriedly locking car doors or clutching a purse more tightly as though expecting to be robbed. Moving to the other side of the sidewalk—or another pew as I experienced in that Salt Lake City church.

THE GAZE

One of the most frequently discussed racial gestures is "the gaze." While White scholars have only recently begun to address "the gaze," Black writers and scholars have been discussing the racial gaze of Whites for decades. What exactly does this term mean? No Black has to ask. But it is hard to put into words for those who have never had to be on the receiving end.

Simply put, it is the look a White person gives a Black person, deliberately or not, when that Black person has the nerve to step into what the White person considers their territory—not just physically but also socially, economically, or politically. It is a look that gives Blacks the ever-present feeling they have to explain or excuse why their bodies are occupying space intended for White people. It is a look that lets the Black person know they don't belong in the White looker's territory, that they are disgusted by the Black person's presence, and in some cases would like to inflict violence to remove the Black person from that space. It is a look of suspicion, disdain, fear, contempt, hostility, or all in one.

When I sat there alone in that Salt Lake City church because White congregants had moved to another pew, their gaze shouted their unspoken disgust at my presence, saying, "This nigger doesn't belong here."

When Trump confronts peaceful Black protestors, a brown-skinned peaceful caravan of Central American refugees, leaders of African nations, a Black former president and his beautiful wife, strong non-White female leaders, his words, facial expressions, body language, gestures, and above all the contempt in his gaze screams his disgust that these interlopers are allowed to occupy the same space as him. Under the condescending, elitist superiority, his glare tells Blacks and Browns: "You SOBs, shithole nations, birther interloping niggers, you have the audacity to think you can consider yourselves equal to ME?"

A familiar axiom is that "the eyes are the windows to the soul," and in this context that is indeed the case. Whites from their position of societal and numerical dominance can say that "the gaze" is harmless. Or as with White Privilege, that it doesn't exist. But Black Americans with a racial memory of the KKK, mob violence, lynching, and other White American oppression feel the burning scald of such a gaze even when White perpetrators are not overtly conscious of exercising it.

Well-known African-American author, feminist scholar, and poet "bell hooks" (spelled lower case, born Gloria Jean Watkins) writes of "the gaze" in terms of the terror she felt in her childhood:

> What did I see in the gazes of those white men who crossed our thresholds that made me afraid, that made black children unable to speak? . . . Their presence terrified me. Whatever their mission, they looked too much like the

unofficial white men who came to enact rituals of terror and torture.

Today that "gaze" still exists, and for too many non-Whites, it evokes those days not so long ago when White Americans had the power and authority to terrorize, torture, and even kill with impunity any "uppity nigger" who dared meet their gaze with any semblance of claiming equality.

The gaze could be seen at last spring's violence in Charlottesville when peaceful protesters of racism were categorized as terrorists while Trump lauded White Supremists displaying Confederate flags and shotguns.

The gaze could be seen when Trump sneered at football players kneeling in solidarity against police brutality, calling them "sons of bitches."

The gaze could be seen when Trump did everything he could to enact the death penalty on fourteen to sixteen year old Black and Hispanic teens known as the Central Park Five and, even after they were cleared of crimes they didn't commit, continues to use his bully pulpit as president to insist they are guilty.

The gaze could be seen in White insurance investment manager Amy Cooper on the now infamous video when she calls the cops on a Black man, falsely claiming he'd assaulted her and threatened her life, because he'd dared ask her to obey the law and put a leash on her dog.

The gaze could be seen from White policeman Derek Chauvin in Missouri, who for over nine minutes refused to take his knee off George Floyd's neck while observers screamed for him to stop. It could be seen in his co-conspirator policemen who simply watched as George Floyd died.

The gaze could be seen in the smirking expression with which Trump watched police firing tear gas and rubber bullets at peaceful protesters so he could stroll across street for a photo op with a Bible on the steps of St. John Episcopal Church. While most of the nation watched appalled at his calloused indifference to human life and civil rights, White Evangelicals hailed his behavior and use of the Bible as a PR prop as doing a "Jericho walk" (Israel's historic march of conquest around Jericho that brought the walls tumbling down; see Joshua 6) and "establishing the Lord's kingdom in the world." Never mind that Jesus said, "My kingdom is not of this world" and that Trump has never claimed to be a follower of Jesus (John 18:36).

The gaze can be seen in White politicians, church leaders, conspiracy theorist talk-show hosts, and right-wing celebrities screaming out invective against peaceful protestors, immigrants, social justice activists, and anyone Black, Brown or White who dares raise a voice or take a stand in opposition to White political, social, or economic interests.

The gaze can be seen in the eyes of White Evangelical ministry leaders who have become multi-millionaires off the donations of God's people even as they invoke God's name on Trump's behalf and pronounce damnation to anyone who dares oppose him or call for accountability.

Whites may truly believe none of these things should be a big deal. But to African Americans experiencing that gaze, they evoke PTSD flashbacks to this kind of rhetoric in the White Evangelical church and this kind of behavior from White government and law enforcement forces that left activists murdered, Martin Luther King assassinated, Black churches bombed, and only too many Black Americans terrorized, in jail, or dead for taking a stand against them.

REVERSE RACISM

Research indicates that many White Evangelicals and Whites in general are not only aware of social, political, and economic gains made by non-Whites but are resentful of these gains. Unbelievably when one looks objectively at the continued statistical gap between America's White population and every other non-White demographic, Blacks in particular, many Whites benefiting most from social and economic privilege are now declaring themselves victims for having to function on a more equal playing field with non-Whites. They use terms like "reverse racism" and decry Affirmative Action.

Where does this idea of victimhood come from? In part, it traces back to the White emphasis on the individual as well as the myth that civil rights gains in the 1960s had erased all remaining inequalities. In other words, since some individual Blacks are prospering more than some individual Whites, the overall social inequalities, including actual social injustices such as in the area of law enforcement, no longer matter. Since this myth assumes that all American demographics are now toeing the same starting line, then any push for continued reform amounts to "special rights" for minority groups rather than a redressing of continued inequality.

Several false assumptions foster White resentment. First, that White Americans, despite their clear continued dominance numerically, socially, economically, and politically, are now an oppressed group. Second, that despite current systemic White Privilege, any further correction of inequalities actually places Whites in danger of victimization.

The third factor in fostering resentment is White denial, which is simply the conscious or unconscious refusal to believe in White Privilege because acknowledging White Privilege would mean acknowledging historic participation in and benefit from unjust social and political systems. It is easier to blame the true victims than risk feelings of guilt and culpability by admitting the reality that one's own group may be enjoying a more fulfilling, economically secure, and materially comfortable life due to the oppression of another group.

The reality is that no one likes to give up power and privilege. When the dominant group in any society is asked to change or to give up something by a "minority" group, it is not surprising that the dominant group assumes the role of preserver of the status quo. The status quo in the United States is socially, politically, and economically advantageous to Whites, and by default in the mind of some Whites, this is precisely as it should be. To be a member of the dominant group is a privilege and not to be given away.

But if a natural and historically common reaction, it is not a Christ-like reaction. Nor is it what God expects to see of His family or in His church. Consider just a few biblical admonitions.

> Do nothing out of selfish ambition or vain conceit. Rather, in humility value others above yourselves, not looking to your own interests but each of you to the interests of the others. In your relationships with one another, have the same mindset as Christ Jesus who, being in very nature God, did not consider equality with God something to be used to his own advantage; rather, he made himself nothing by taking the very nature of a servant. (Philippians 2:3-7)

> Let no one seek his own good, but the good of his neighbor. (1 Corinthians 10:24)

So in everything, do to others what you would have them do to you, for this sums up the Law and the Prophets. (Matthew 7:12)

You, my brothers and sisters, were called to be free. But do not use your freedom to indulge the flesh; rather, serve one another humbly in love. For the entire law is fulfilled in keeping this one command: "Love your neighbor as yourself." (Galatians 5:13-14)

Which brings us back to our core topic—the White Evangelical church in America and what its role has been in all the above over the last four hundred-plus years since those calling themselves followers of Jesus Christ first arrived on the American continent.

CHAPTER SEVEN

DIVIDED BY FAITH

To what extent can White Evangelical Americans be held at minimum complicit in systematic racism and discrimination of the African-American community? Simple statistics paint a stark picture. Thanks to the various Great Revivals and Awakenings, during the nineteenth century an estimated fifty percent of Americans and eighty-five percent of Protestants identified as Evangelicals. White Evangelicalism was overwhelmingly the core identity of the American church, especially in the South.

Which means that the White Evangelical church would have a hard time claiming that their leadership and membership had clean hands in propagating slavery, Jim Crow, segregation, and other elements of African-American discrimination. Rev. Martin Luther King Jr. in his final book *Where Do We Go From Here: Chaos or Community?* went further to state that the White Evangelical church "has been an accomplice in structuring racism into the architecture of American society."

Nor can racism be dismissed as just a problem of White Southerners. The first independent Black denomination, the African Methodist Episcopal (AME.) Church, had its origins in 1787 after White congregants yanked its founders, Richard Allen and Absalom Jones, from their knees because they had dared to pray in a Whites-only section of Philadelphia's St. George's Methodist Episcopal Church.

After the Civil War, many Northern African-American Christian groups such as the AME carried out missionary outreach in the South, planting church congregations that connected newly-freed African-American Christians with African-American denominations of the North. By 1870, the AME denomination had grown significantly. In urban areas after the 1870s, there was a large push towards multi-denominational evangelism with both White and African-American congregations. This was the time period of great evangelists like Dwight L. Moody and Billy Sunday.

But this was also the time that African Americans began more than ever to form their own church denominations, in part because of the unequal treatment they were receiving in integrated church denominations in both the North and the South. White Christian theology was often used to justify this split with the implication that it was God's plan to have people separated by race. In the South, churches were segregated by government decree. In the North they were equally segregated by choice.

Let's examine the Church of God (Anderson, Indiana) as just one example chosen out of many similar ones. Birthed out of Pentecostal revivals in Michigan and Indiana during the 1880s, the denomination's original message was the unity of all believers regardless of race or ethnicity. No specific stance was taken on race relations. Both Blacks and Whites responded to the preaching of the Gospel and were accepted into the denomination.

Congregations remained largely segregated, in part because Black and White congregants lived in different communities. But some church leaders were advocating for full inclusion of Blacks into churches and speaking out against racial prejudice. In violation of segregation laws, White and Black Church of God members also held worship and business meetings together throughout the southern United States, including the annual Camp Meetings.

That said, more than a casual uneasiness about racial integration existed among some leaders and members. On September 2, 1897, an editorial in the denomination's primary publication, the *Gospel Trumpet,* stated:

We do not believe in White and Colored people mixing together in marriage or in any other way that is unnecessary. We believe it would be better if it were convenient to have it so that they meet in separate meetings. But there are places where it is almost necessary for them to meet together, and they do in many places meet harmoniously and to the glory of God. I have been in meetings in both North and South, even in Augusta, Georgia, where both White and colored brethren met together in harmony and unity, God having swept away the prejudice from their hearts . . . There is nothing wrong in them meeting separately where it can be done to the glory of God. Or on the other hand there is nothing wrong in them meeting together where it can be done to the glory of God.

Sadly, as time went on the Church of God gave into social pressures toward segregated congregations. In 1912, White leaders at the annual Camp Meeting "suggested to the Blacks that they might find it more desirable if they found some other place to worship." The request caused deep sadness among Black members and led to a lasting change in what had been cordial interracial relations. While the Church of God remained one denomination at national level, it became segregated at the local church level. Some Black leaders eventually did break away to form their own ministerial association and an independent Black satellite national structure.

By the mid-1950s, the General Ministerial Assembly of the Church of God was feeling pressure from Black leaders for broader involvement in the larger denomination. A commission was created to investigate the problem of segregation within the denomination. In 1961, the commission made a series of recommendations to encourage integration at national and local levels, closing with the following admonition: "This, therefore, is the time to take heart and practice the message we have taught."

By the late 1960s, the Church of God had provided seminars and workshops about racial integration and had taken action to integrate national boards. In 1971, the Executive Council of the Church of God elected Marcus H. Morgan as its first Black chairperson.

This denominational history of the Church of God with regard to race is given simply to demonstrate the complexity of the relationship between Christianity and the maintenance of White Supremacy. The history of many Evangelical denominations follows a similar pattern. What becomes clear is that when the church is not openly advocating for a change in the structures of society, its silence results in a de facto support of the status quo.

THE CIVIL RIGHTS ERA

During the Civil Rights Movement, African-American churchgoers used their presence in church to unite people on civil rights issues. This was significantly more successful in the South than in the North as Southern problems of legal segregation were easier to identify and fix in comparison to their Northern counterparts who confronted more covert issues such as urban minority ghettos. African-American church members and leaders played a large role in the Civil Rights Movement, which also gave the movement distinct religious undertones. Appealing to the public using religious reasoning and doctrine was common. Black churches also became an important base for social organizing and community outreach.

At the beginning of the Civil Rights Era, there was some effort from White Evangelicals to integrate churches. This push ended as White Americans showed little interest in pushing for social segregation. In fact, the Civil Rights Era saw a major White backlash against Black progress. Still, many historians have noted that Christian faith was an important motivator in whether White Americans were in favor of civil rights since a majority of Christians believed racism was sinful. This varied widely by region as Southern pastors were substantially more racist than their Northern counterparts.

At the same time, many White Evangelicals who believed racism to be wrong felt that striving for integration and equality was pointless and even impossible because the world was descending into chaos as a precursor to "the Second Coming" of Jesus as described in the Book of Revelation. In the 1970s and 1980s, many White Evangelical ministry leaders and authors like Hal Lindsey, Jack van Impe, and Salem Kirban popularized in books, movies, and from the pulpit the assurance that the Second Coming was not only imminent but would definitely happen before the end of the century. Why bother to speak out or take action on issues like social justice or even pollution, the environment, energy crisis, or any other "earthly" problems when the planet wouldn't be around much longer anyway?

In 2000, White Evangelical sociologists Michael Emerson and Christian Smith published their intensive study titled *Divided By Faith* on the relationship between race and religion, specifically Evangelical Christianity, in the United States. *Divided By Faith* is still one of the most influential books on the topic, in part because of the extensive nature of the investigation based on national survey data of Evangelical Protestants across the United States. Emerson and Smith concluded from their study that the United States must be understood as a "racialized society." In other words, a society where race matters profoundly for differences in life experiences, opportunities, and social relationships.

Emerson and Smith also established the historical role White Evangelical Christianity has played in justifying the racialization of American society from the eighteenth century to the mid-twentieth century. In blunt terms, White Evangelical Christianity has done very little to bring about actual racial equality. On the contrary, it has been utilized as a mechanism for justifying racial attitudes and establishing White Supremacy. Emerson and Smith demonstrate how the very organization and development of American Evangelicalism has been the driving force behind the homogenization of White Christian groups, both through racially segregated worship and the emphasis that racism is an individual, not societal, problem, so does not need to be addressed by the church as a whole.

There is no suggestion in this study that any of these outcomes were designed with malice or deliberate intent. On the contrary, Emerson and Smith sum up their book as:

A story of how well-intentioned people, their values, and their institutions actually recreate racial divisions and inequalities they ostensibly oppose.

The solution Emerson and Smith proposed was simple: the multi-cultural church. The concept being that if the various races worshipped together, reconciliation and understanding would follow. Whether or not this is the solution is hard to judge since twenty years after the publication of *Divided by Faith*, the growth of multi-cultural churches, defined as at least one in five members being from another ethnicity than the dominant race, has only risen from six percent to sixteen percent. A high percentage of these are mega-churches where congregations are so large that different racial groups can easily avoid each other. Even at that, an eighty-percent White ratio means those of other ethnicities are simply joining a White-culture church rather than any real multi-cultural blend. Smaller congregations remain overwhelmingly homogeneous.

One of Cincinnati's most recognizable and senior church pastors, Rev. Damon Lynch Jr., states that the racial climate today is more toxic than fifty years ago while racial attitudes both in and outside of the church have hardened. He says too many White ministers and churchgoers still believe Whites are superior to African Americans.

"We've been at this for what seems like forever," says Rev. Lynch, who in September 2020 will begin his forty-eighth year as pastor of New Jerusalem Baptist Church in Carthage. "The will is just not there for White Evangelicals and White clergy to address racism."

Ironically, a recent Pew Study reveals that African-Americans are today the most likely of any racial group in the United States to belong to a church congregation. A 2019 Barna Group study commissioned by the American Bible Society reveals that African Americans are the ethnic group most likely to use the Bible at least three to four times a week (69%), compared to a 44% of Whites and 52% of Hispanics. African Americans are also more likely to report life transformation as a result of their Bible use than Whites and more commonly believe the Bible is the actual Word of God. African Americans engage with their faith more regularly and report finding greater fulfillment in their faith than Whites.

CHAPTER EIGHT

A CHRISTIAN NATION?

W as America ever a Christian nation? Much less, a White Evangelical nation? And why should this matter either way? It matters because the current White Evangelical crusade to "take our country back" and "make America great again" is based on the assumption that:

- One, America ever was a Christian nation versus a nation with many Christians in it.

- Two, that any nation clear back to fourth century Roman emperor Constantine instituting Christianity as the Roman Empire's state religion has ever truly been a Christian nation versus a nation with state-imposed Christian worship.

A bigger issue is whether God's Word even teaches that a political goal for Christians should be to "make" their country Christian. In fact, Scripture is clear on this point. Only two "nations" are referenced in the Bible as God's nations. In the Old Testament, that nation is Israel, the only nation in history established specifically as a nation chosen and ruled by God. The second "nation" in the New Testament is the church, as the apostle Peter laid out clearly in his first epistle:

> But you are a chosen people, a royal priesthood, a holy nation, God's special possession, that you may declare the praises of him who called you out of darkness into his wonderful light. Once you were not a people, but now you are the people of God. (1 Peter 2:9-10)

This passage does not reference a specific geopolitical entity within physical borders but the global body of Christ, the Church, made up of Christians from countless tribes and tongues and nations who worship God. While it is certainly acceptable to state that secular nations have varying degrees of Christian influence, it is biblically unacceptable to refer to any nation other than Israel and the Church as nations of God.

We can say that the United States had strong Christian influences during its founding. We can state the historical reality that most of its White settlers came from countries that by law enforced Christianity on its citizens and punished, often by death, the practice of other forms of religion, including other Christian dogmas not legislated by the current government. During the formative years of White settlement of America, nations with state-mandated Christianity like Britain, France, and Spain alternated between Protestant regimes jailing and murdering Catholics and Catholic regimes jailing and murdering Protestants.

Of British, French, and Spanish colonists migrating to the New World, only a fraction of groups such as the Pilgrims, French Huguenots, Quakers, and Puritans came for religious freedom. By far the majority of new arrivals came to take advantage of land grants and rumors of gold, or they came as slaves or indentured servants. Even in the New World, religious groups like the Puritans and Anglican Church levied fines, jailed, and otherwise persecuted anyone within the boundaries of their political control practicing another form of Christian faith. Colonies like Pennsylvania and Maryland were founded as religious havens for minority Christian groups like the Quakers and Catholics, who could not live or worship freely in other colonies controlled by Anglican or Puritan state churches.

The clause in the Constitution guaranteeing separation of church and state was not intended to protect churches from the state or Christianity from other religions. Ironically, its purpose was to protect Christian citizens from being persecuted by other Christian citizens for daring to worship the Christian God in a different manner and in a different church setting. If a majority of colonists attended church, this reflected more the penalties imposed by religious and governmental authorities for non-attendance than genuine devout faith in God. Another reason why the Constitution guaranteed a secular rather than religious society as a basic human right and freedom.

This is not merely a matter of semantics. A monumental shift has happened over the last half century in the dynamic of White Evangelical relations with the rest of American society. That shift has its origin in the myth of an original "Golden Age" when America was a "Christian nation." White Evangelicals endlessly quote God's promise to King Solomon—or more specifically to the nation of Israel:

If my people, which are called by my name, shall humble themselves, and pray, and seek my face, and turn from their wicked ways; then will I hear from heaven, and will forgive their sin, and will heal their land. (2 Chronicles 7:14)

The premise of White Evangelicals in quoting this passage is that "my people" is not referring to the actual followers of God, the body of Christ, the Church, but to America as a geopolitical entity. This is a significant theological error because it permits White Evangelicals to divide all of society into "us" vs. "them." Whatever problem in America is the fault of "them"—i.e., the abortionists, homosexuals, liberals, feminists, secular humanists, evolutionists, mainstream media, or anyone who dares vote for a politician or party not endorsed by White Evangelical leadership. If only all "them" would humble themselves, pray, and turn from their wicked ways, America would be restored to its Golden Age.

The problem is that neither God nor this passage is calling on the geopolitical entity called the United States of America to repent in order to see God's forgiveness and healing. Rather, it is God's people who are being called to repent. And that means the Church. The problem is not "them" but "us." After all, Christians teach that it is impossible to live a righteous life without having been regenerated by the Holy Spirit. Why then should we be surprised that sinners are acting like sinners? Why should we demand that sinners stop acting like sinners in order to heal our land?

In truth, the problem isn't that sinners are acting like a bunch of sinners but that the Church is acting like a bunch of sinners. This makes the culture war a completely misguided preoccupation. Instead of assigning blame, White Evangelicals should be soul-searching.

Instead of talking about how displeased God is with enemies of Christian culture, they should be sharing God's love and grace with them. Instead of trying to "win America back," they should be trying to get back to the heart of God.

The results of these mistakes are predictable and evident. The White Evangelical church has continued to live in a way that estranges them from Jesus's commands. They have created deep wells of antagonism toward the very people they are supposed to be pointing to Christ. If their "prosperity gospel" teaches that success is proof of God's favor, then their complete lack of progress in winning the "culture war" must indicate that God finds their approach in "taking back our country" repugnant.

The core of this is not about spreading the gospel and seeing people come to know Jesus Christ. It goes back to the simple motive of maintaining the historical position of White power and dominance. The perennial drumbeat of the religious right has been that White Evangelicals are losing power within American society and something needs done to win it back.

Recent decades have seen an ever more clamorous cry from White Evangelicals with ever greater zeal and harsher condemnation to "win America back." But in all the clamor and effort to regain political and cultural power, few White Evangelical voices have bothered asking whether winning secular power should have been the goal in the first place or whether a tattered and soiled reputation for Christ's bride was a fair price to pay for a failed attempt to grasp political and social power.

THE MORAL MAJORITY

Perhaps one of the loudest voices in the war to regain White Evangelical political and social power has been the Moral Majority, as

Southern White Evangelical televangelist Jerry Falwell christened his conservative right-wing political machine. Falwell explained his reason for this name.

> I was convinced that there was a moral majority out there among those more than two hundred million Americans sufficient in number to turn back the flood tide of moral permissiveness, family breakdown and general capitulation to evil and to foreign policies such as Marxism Leninism.

Falwell's "moral majority" represented an important shift. Notice that he wasn't trying to recruit just White Evangelicals or even those who identified themselves as Christians. He was pursuing a broader coalition that would include anyone in agreement that:

- There was a general breakdown of morality and family structure in America.

- Communism should be opposed.

- America was becoming more evil.

There is nothing intrinsically wrong with casting a wide net in attempting to gain political power. The pitfall is when a Christian ministry leader does it in a manner that closely identifies the political effort with religious belief. A major pitfall is when people stop identifying Christianity as those who are making a concerted effort to be followers of Christ to those who agree with a few general propositions about moral breakdown, communism, and evil in society. This becomes an even bigger problem when Christian leadership begins demanding allegiance to their particular political entity as evidence of Christian faith.

This is exactly what has happened over the last few decades. The label "Moral Majority" speaks volumes. It projects someone pursuing power (dominion), not faithfulness to a way of life that requires sacrifice and self-denial. It implies the building of a political coalition to acquire earthly influence. When Jesus spoke of building His kingdom, He said:

> Enter through the narrow gate. For wide is the gate and broad is the road that leads to destruction, and many enter through it. But small is the gate and narrow the road that leads to life, and only a few find it. (Matthew 7:13-14)

In these verses, our Lord and Savior depicts the Church, not as a "Moral Majority" dominating a nation, but as a rebellion against the status quo of evil—or a resistance movement. In compliance with the will of the Master, Christ's followers are working in enemy territory and their numbers are few, but they continue their brave fight to win as many to their cause as possible. Contrast this with today's White Evangelical leaders who publicly denounce brothers and sisters in Christ as sinners and even having lost their salvation if they don't vote for whichever politicians/party they've decided best represent their hope of regaining temporal power—regardless of how immoral and ungodly those politicians/party may be.

The tragic irony of the "Moral Majority" approach is that the Bible does speak of the followers of Christ being influential in society. The "small gate" statement occurred well into in Jesus's Sermon on the

Mount (Matthew 5-7). Earlier in the Sermon on the Mount, Jesus said to his followers:

> You are the salt of the earth. But if the salt loses its saltiness, how can it be made salty again? It is no longer good for anything, except to be thrown out and trampled underfoot. You are the light of the world. A town built on a hill cannot be hidden. Neither do people light a lamp and put it under a bowl. Instead they put it on its stand, and it gives light to everyone in the house. In the same way, let your light shine before others, that they may see your good deeds and glorify your Father in heaven. (Matthew 5:13-16)

What Jesus was saying here was that godly influence would not be achieved by the accumulation of earthly power and authority but through living a life of Christlikeness that projected the light and very flavor of true Christianity to a watching world. In fact, when Jesus Himself had the most reason to exercise earthly authority to save Himself from the cross, He flatly told Pontius Pilate that His kingdom was not one of earthly power or force.

> Jesus said, "My kingdom is not of this world. If it were, my servants would fight to prevent my arrest by the Jewish leaders. But now my kingdom is from another place." (John 18:36)

If Jesus had wanted to attain earthly power as we typically understand it, He already had the means and power to do so within

His grasp as He told Peter rebukingly just a few hours earlier when Peter tried to stop Jesus's arrest by wielding a sword:

> Put your sword back in its place . . . Do you think I cannot call on my Father, and he will at once put at my disposal more than twelve legions of angels? But how then would the Scriptures be fulfilled that say it must happen in this way?" (Matthew 26:52-54)

But Jesus's mission was not the accumulation of such power. We are given a clear picture of His mission in one of the most familiar and memorized passages in Scripture:

> For God so loved the world, that He gave His only begotten Son, that whoever believes in Him shall not perish, but have eternal life. For God did not send the Son into the world to judge the world, but **that the world through Him might be saved**. (John 3:16, 17)

The mission on which Jesus came to earth was not the accumulation of temporal power but the people's redemption! A mission that can only be accomplished in the Spirit and by following the example of humility Jesus Himself displayed washing the disciples' feet (John 13). This is a humility that looks first to serve people, not lord over them. It is a humility that takes the lesser seat rather than demanding to be at the head of the table. It is an approach that is not concerned with the accumulation of earthly power but the regeneration and spiritual maturing of body of Christ through the

Great Commission, as proclaimed by our Lord at the close of Matthew's gospel:

> Then Jesus came to them and said, "All authority in heaven and on earth has been given to me. Therefore go and make disciples of all nations, baptizing them in the name of the Father and of the Son and of the Holy Spirit, and teaching them to obey everything I have commanded you. And surely I am with you always, to the very end of the age. (Matthew 28:18-20)

The power to complete this mission was delegated by Jesus to His disciples. By extension, the Church has been given authority and power from Christ to accomplish its given mission. In light of this, White Evangelical pursuit of political power in the name of "taking America back" is not merely a misunderstanding of the mission Christ gave the Church but a rebuke to Christ that the power and authority He gave the Church is not sufficient to do the job.

The focus of the Church was never intended to be the accumulation of earthly power or the subduing of a secular nation. The mission given by Christ concerns the redemption of souls and instruction in the way of Christ that leads to abundant living.

The White Evangelical pursuit of a culture war that has basically turned Christian politics into a hostile, angry "us" versus "them" represents a loss of vision regarding the mission that Christ gave the church. It has alienated the very people they were supposed to be bringing into the body of Christ through a loving presentation of the gospel and demonstration of Christlikeness. It has also failed on its own merits, i.e., in "taking America back." This is undoubtedly because such a war is in no way empowered by Christ, who finds the whole endeavor misguided and counterproductive. We know this because of the extent to which such an effort contradicts the words Christ spoke.

Bottom line, the base fear that motivates this war is loss of power while the base passion spurring it on is the regaining of power. This is made to sound more palatable and spiritual by the constant refrain that White Evangelicals are "winning America back for God." It is just a happy coincidence that getting America back for God also represents an increase in power, authority, and influence for White Evangelicals themselves.

The Pharisees of Jesus's day fretted that they would lose "both our place and our nation" (John 11:48). Sadly, that became the ultimate motive for plotting Christ's murder on the cross. For the last few decades, White Evangelicals have publicly, stridently, angrily, and unlovingly fought to regain their place of power and dominance in their nation. They have used non-Christian means in an attempt to achieve that resurgence of power. The outcome of such unbiblical behavior has been the same as it was in Jesus's day: "Jesus left and hid himself from them" (John 8:59).

America was not, is not, and cannot be a Christian nation. White Evangelical claims to the contrary are historically ignorant and biblically unfounded. The desire to return to a past era has far more to do with the loss of sociopolitical and cultural power than with a longing for an era of genuine Christlikeness which in fact never existed. Dear White brothers and sisters, with deep love and sorrow I must speak out that your pursuit of power in this way has plugged up the well of God's love and mercy to countless Americans in need of the gospel truth but who now associate White Evangelicals most strongly with being anti-abortion and anti-homosexual rather than being pro-grace and pro-mercy.

CHAPTER NINE

DEMYTHICIZING

THE ORIGIN STORY

So how did the myth of a Golden Age of deep committed Christian faith in America ever take hold among White Evangelicals? Certainly not during early centuries of European settlement of the Americas. The emphasis then was on breaking free from state-mandated forms of Christianity and establishing a secular society where all could worship freely as they chose. It was not Puritanism that dominated the world view of the Founding Fathers but the Enlightenment and Renaissance.

Like most Americans of the time, the majority of the Founding Fathers had been baptized into one of the mainline churches as infants and in public/political discourse evoked a generalized Providence. But many had minimal church affiliation or attendance as adults. Quite a number, including George Washington and Thomas Jefferson, considered themselves Deists and enlightened Humanists.

In other words, they believed some general deity had created the world, but not necessarily the Christian God. They believed that reason and science should control human behavior, not religion. Wording in their writings such as Providence, Creator, Divine Goodness rather than evoking Jesus or God were indicators of Deist beliefs.

In fact, it was not until 1954 that the words "under God" were added to the Pledge of Allegiance. It was 1956 when "In God We Trust" was added to American currency. It is this time period of the 1950s that most evokes nostalgia in White Evangelicals when they echo the myth of a "Christian America." In a nation recovering from the horrors of two world wars, there was indeed a surge in church membership from 57 percent of the American population in 1950 to 63.3 percent in 1960. On any given Sunday in this decade, almost half of the American population could be found in a church.

What brought about such a movement? Certainly a much-needed revival and turning to God after the horror, violence, and licentiousness that accompanied two world wars. But there was also a renewed social pressure that if one was to be considered a good citizen, much more so to garner votes as a civic or political leader, church membership—rather than any genuine faith—was a must.

President Eisenhower himself, the president who brought "under God" and "in God we trust" into the public arena, believed in a vague non-denominational God but had never been a church goer. Once in the White House, he was pressured to join a church. He chose the National Presbyterian Church in Washington, DC but quickly became frustrated at the pastor's lack of discretion.

In one well-documented comment to his press secretary, Eisenhower exploded: "You go and tell that goddam minister that if he gives out one more story about my religious faith, I won't join his goddam church!" This is the "Golden Age" to which White Evangelicals long to return!

BILLY GRAHAM

But many would attribute the introduction of White Evangelicalism into the public arena to a single man—a young evangelist named Billy Graham. Graham was "born again" in 1934 at a tent revival and later attended Wheaton College, a Christian university, where he met his wife Ruth Bell, a daughter of medical missionaries serving in China. After serving several years as a pastor, Graham became an evangelist for Youth for Christ, a parachurch organization that emphasized both Christianity and patriotism in urging people toward Christ, an emphasis that influenced Graham's own evangelistic message.

Graham spoke to American hopes and anxieties, including nationalism, communism, and materialism, with the simple message that accepting Christ as one's personal savior was the answer to all evil in the world. Known as the father of modern evangelicalism, Graham preached in person to over two hundred million people during his career as well as founding numerous Christian media outlets such as the leading evangelical magazine *Christianity Today* and his *Hour of Decision* radio broadcast.

Graham became religious advisor to numerous presidents from Harry Truman all the way to Barack Obama. But he refused to take political sides and very pointedly refused to join the Moral Majority, pointing out strongly:

> I'm for morality, but morality goes beyond sex to human freedom and social justice . . . Evangelists cannot be closely

identified with any particular party or person. We have to stand in the middle in order to preach to all people, right and left.

To give Billy Graham credit he amply deserves, he was among the first White Southern Evangelicals to integrate his evangelistic crusades, famously on one occasion ripping down the ropes that divided "Whites Only" and "Black" sections of the stadiums where he preached. That said, he disapproved of Civil Rights protests and sit-ins and refused to weigh in on social justice issues. In answer to Martin Luther King's often-quoted statement of hope that a day would come in Alabama when Black children could walk hand in hand with White children, Graham famously responded that this could happen only after Jesus Christ returned to earth to establish His kingdom.

Billy Graham's emphasis on the personal conversion of individuals as the overarching goal of the Great Commission left out any consideration of social responsibility for the Christian. A typical sermon would present current societal ills, focusing especially on common fears such as high crime, communism, the Cold War, nuclear threat, political and social unrest (including the Civil Rights Movement!). All painting a picture of a world in deep crisis that might in any moment be destroyed. The only solution to avoid being part of that destruction was personal repentance of sins and turning to a personal relationship with Jesus Christ.

Again, there is nothing intrinsically wrong with calling people to repentance and faith in Jesus Christ. Nor is there any arguing that Jesus Himself taught that God's kingdom would be built through the "yeast" of the gospel (Matthew 13:33) as more and more individuals were transformed by the power of the Holy Spirit and living lives of

Christlikeness. But what this emphasis obscured was the extent to which communal ills and unjust governmental policies contributed to the problems Graham decried.

In Graham's evangelicalism, the individual was the cause of all the world's problems, so changing the individual was all that was needed to solve them. He saw no need for communities, peoples, or even the body of Christ to work together to address societal wrongs. In fact, he expressed grave concern that the "social gospel" was liberal humanism while liberation theology, which considered oppressive governments as sinful structures the gospel could and should confront, was incompatible with biblical evangelism.

All this was in contrast to the social reform movements of the late nineteenth and early twentieth centuries when White Evangelicals were deeply involved in organized campaigns to legislate reforms of such things as child labor, slum housing, the sex trade, drug and alcohol use, and general promotion of Christian morals. White Evangelicals of that era believed that transforming America through social reform to a nation that increasingly reflected Christian principles not only fulfilled America's "exceptional" role in the world but was part of ushering in God's kingdom globally. One popular evangelical politician, William Jennings Bryan, spoke openly of "the destiny of the United States to guide the world morally."

What brought about such a change? When did White Evangelicals decide that working toward social reform, at least those that benefited their own people, was not biblical? It is a bit of a simplification of a complex question, but the commencement of World War 1 was perhaps the most clearly identifiable dividing point.

The optimism voiced by William Jennings Bryan that social reform movements could improve the lot and character of American citizens gave way to a militant America united against the "un-American other." This was a Great War of the righteous, chosen people of God fighting for the "American Way" against the unrighteous, un-American enemy. Christianity and American nationalism became synonymous. As famed evangelist of the era Billy Sunday put it: "Christianity and Patriotism are synonymous terms, and hell and traitors are synonymous."

The Great War shifted the focus from bringing about American exceptionalism through social reform to making it a battle of true Americans, i.e., White Evangelicals, against the un-American. The rise of communism in Russia and China and related fears created a panic that polarized the nation. Every social reform movement from women's suffrage and safe working conditions to fair wages and civil rights was labeled as "communist" and "un-American" by corporate business interests and political factions that benefited by unbridled capitalism, unregulated industry and exploitation of resources, and cheap labor.

This narrative fed right into a White Evangelical mindset, above all in the South, that had used similar rhetoric and fear of the Black "other" to justify segregation, Jim Crow, and Black Codes. As Christian denominations competed for the claim of being the most "true-blooded American," the churches with the strongest anti-Communist and anti-immigrant message were the winners. It is notable that we are hearing the exact same rhetoric in our current election cycle with the political opposition being routinely castigated as "other" and "communist" while the fanning of the flames against immigrants comes right out of a 1920s White Supremist political play book.

Throughout the twentieth century, White Evangelicals have framed American history in terms of American exceptionalism and as a nation with a special covenant with God while viewing themselves as a "faithful remnant" fighting against America's cultural and political decay. Ironically, they separated themselves from taking any further active role in social improvement. Yet at the same time, they have called for the restoration of a "Christian America" through the seizing of political power.

American White Evangelicals have repeatedly propagated the myth that America not only should be a Christian nation but also that it had always been one. Since communism is essentially an atheistic philosophy, American institutions began openly promoting religion as a strategic tool to combat communism. This was a battle White Evangelicals were winning, as evidenced by the spike in church attendance during the 1950s. Then came the cultural upheavals and social unrest of the 1960s and 1970s, which White Evangelicals framed as a battle for the American soul.

As White Evangelicals began feeling under attack by the secular world, they adopted increasingly aggressive and defensive tactics to "reshape social life in America," which they saw as morally compromised by liberation movements. Rather than even consider the objective merits of various social justice issues, White Evangelicals posited a return to a mythic Christian past. Jerry Falwell's "I love America" rallies were among the movements that helped reinvigorate the myth of America's "holy history" as a Christian nation. That this past they lauded was hardly an improvement for Blacks and other minorities, the disadvantaged, or half the population—women—who had as few civil rights as Blacks in this mythical "better America," was swept under the rug.

INDIVIDUALISM AND WHITE EVANGELICALS

Research demonstrates that White Americans as a whole see race largely from an individualist perspective. To take this one step further, White Evangelicals as a whole see religion from an individualist perspective. This is not necessarily a negative or a positive but simply a cultural characteristic. In examining cultures globally, the American culture is one of the most highly individualistic cultures on earth while many African and Asian cultures come in at the opposite end of the culture spectrum as emphasizing "collectivism" or "community." In other words, placing the emphasis on the needs, desires, and opinions of the community above those of the individual.

In Evangelical Christianity, an individualistic emphasis is likewise placed on making a personal decision to follow God and having a personal relationship with Jesus Christ. This is in contrast with many other religions and even branches of Christianity such as Catholicism and Eastern Orthodoxy where a child is baptized into their religious affiliation as an infant and is expected to remain in that affiliation as part of their cultural heritage and to be considered part of the larger community.

In summation, it can't be overestimated how much the American heritage of individualism has contributed to attitudes of White Evangelicals in explaining away racism and inequality in terms of individualistic traits and achievement. If racism still exists, they argue, these are the acts of a few ignorant individuals. If inequality still exists, this is simply because individuals from racial minorities don't try hard enough.

In the context of religion, this also translates into how White Evangelicals see being a good person or good citizen as something accomplished by individuals. Being good means being a moral person, honest citizen, hardworking employee, and helping other individuals in need. Again, these are all good things, and no one is denying the importance of personal accountability and responsibility. But this individualism allows White Evangelicals to disconnect themselves from social responsibilities and the problems created by the racialization of society.

Research done by Emerson and Smith for their seminal title on this topic, *Divided by Faith*, indicates that most White Evangelical congregations see their public role as forming good, law-abiding, God-worshipping, moral individual citizens. The same research data showed a core belief that an individual can be a good person and good Christian with little if any awareness of the participation their community, family, or even church may have in oppressive, unjust socio-political systems.

Well-known White Evangelical author Philip Yancey speaks biographically in his writings of growing up in a White Evangelical southern church in the 1950s where he was taught that the Klu Klux Klan was "a last line of defense to preserve the Christian purity of the South" and that desegregation and John Kennedy were assaults on Christian liberty. The hypocrisy of those teachings coming from Christian leaders and the social injustices he witnessed pushed him into his own crisis of faith as a young adult.

For most White Evangelicals, good comes from individual morality, active citizenship, and acts of kindness. In another research study, the Pew Forum on Religious and Public Life, White Evangelicals overwhelmingly believe that "with hard work most people can get ahead." This belief places all responsibility for success or failure on the individual for their life circumstances while ignoring the influence of systemic oppression.

JUST WHITE ENTITLEMENTS

This same attitude fosters not just a White Evangelical disconnect from social responsibility in general but a specific belief that God rewards those who are faithful. A biblical truth, of course (Romans

2:6; 1 Corinthians 15:58; Galatians 6:9; Colossians 3:23-24), but in this situation taken out of context. The White Evangelical myth, strongly tied to the prosperity gospel, teaches that those who enjoy good fortune have earned it through strong faith—and conversely the logical extrapolation that those who don't enjoy good fortune simply haven't earned it and therefore don't deserve it.

The prosperity gospel, which teaches that it is always God's will for believers to be financially prosperous (never mind that neither Jesus, His apostles, nor those who took His gospel around the world, often under conditions of extreme persecution, ever pursued financial prosperity!), was popularized by televangelists like Pat Robertson, Jim Baker, Jimmy Swaggart, and others. In what Pat Robertson has called the "law of reciprocity," this belief suggests that individuals, groups, communities, and populations are given what they deserve. So those who are not blessed with equal prosperity have clearly done or are doing something which offends God. In other words, social realities such as poverty are the result of personal problems or weaknesses caused by spiritual ineptitude and lack of faith.

This perspective in turn allows White Evangelicals to believe their socio-political advantage is something they've earned while ignoring any considerations of systemic oppression and injustice. This is especially true among denominations that hold to strong Calvinist tenets of predestination, which hold that God has already predetermined who will be saved and that all others are born predestined for hell without hope or choice. Such beliefs engendered in Calvinists a deep-seated need to be sure they were among the "elect" destined for heaven, so they began looking at financial success as proof of God's favor.

To go one step further, Calvinists came to the conclusion that people groups, whether globally or within their own American communities, who were enduring poverty, starvation, oppression, or social injustice must be suffering because God had predestined them to that abuse due to their own bad conduct or lack of faith. As a group, God has doomed them to hell. So why should Christians concern themselves with the social well-being of people God has already rejected and destined for a lower social status?

Calvinists are also the most likely to raise the old "sons of Ham" (identified as Blacks) serving "sons of Shem" (identified as Whites) heresy as excuse for social inequality. It is no coincidence that the Dutch Reform Afrikaners who created and imposed apartheid in South Africa were staunch Calvinists. As one White Evangelical pastor told a friend of mine when broached as to how a God who calls His followers to love could create a majority of human beings predestined to hell from birth without hope or choice:

> I will admit I've always wondered how it is that God's followers so often exhibit more love and care for the lost than the God who created them. But that is what Scripture teaches, and it is not for us to question what God has predestined.

This perspective has been the subject of questions and discussions within Black Christian churches and communities for many years. In his book *Is God a White Racist? A Preamble to Black Theology,* African-American minister and Yale professor of religious philosophy William Jones argued that given the history of Blacks and Whites in America, some kind of "divine racism" must apply unless one's theology encompasses human free will and choice of action that results in conditions such as slavery or freedom, whether individually or as a group.

The irony is that the tenets of White Evangelical prosperity gospel would suggest that the Babylonian, Assyrian, Persian, Roman, Chinese, Indian, Russian, and other empires that enjoyed lavish prosperity and power for centuries on end were by definition more righteous than, say, the nation of Israel or people of God—much more so the countless martyrs of the early church, including Christ's own apostles. But this is indeed how certain high-profile White Evangelicals explain tragic events, whether in the lives of individuals or communities.

Franklin Graham was quoted as proclaiming Hurricane Katrina to be a sign of God's wrath on New Orleans, a city with a majority Black population, because of its wickedness. That the drug and alcohol use, sexual immorality, and other examples of New Orleans evils Graham cites differ minimally from every other major American city gives no reason why God should intervene personally to strike a majority-Black city versus countless equally sinful majority-White cities. I have to wonder if Graham is currently denouncing a majority-White America as being smitten by God for its wickedness since the COVID-19 pandemic is hitting the United States worse than other any nation!

CHAPTER TEN

NATIONAL ASSOCIATION

OF EVANGELICALS

A s much as White Evangelicals celebrated American history as a powerful narrative of individual liberty and religious freedom, they resisted social changes that threatened to undo American traditions. Specifically, a status quo in which they were dominant. This myth laid the groundwork for the political action of White Evangelicals, particularly resolutions made by the National Association of Evangelicals, a leading Evangelical organization, in post-World War 2 resurgence of Evangelicalism.

In truth, the organization would be better termed the National Association of White Evangelicals as, while not intentionally segregated, its leadership and stated purposes centered solely around the perspective and political positions of White Evangelicals.

The NAE postulated a concern that secularism would replace America's Christian character, thereby diminishing its claim to exceptionalism. Their strongest targets were the judiciary for having ruled from the bench in banning state-sanctioned imposition of one specific religion in a public forum. Specifically, Christian prayer or solely Christian prayer and/or religious education within the public school system or other government-funded institutions. If America was indeed a Christian nation, then American Christians had a right and even duty to fight to keep other religions or neutral secularism out of the schools, government offices, and other public forums.

The judiciary had not in any way ruled against Christian religious freedom. Rather, it had ruled that America was a secular nation where every religion had equal right to be exercised and where non-Christians had equal rights to keep their children from being indoctrinated in the dominant religion—or even a particular brand of Christianity such as Protestantism versus Catholic. To the White Evangelical establishment, this was not a matter of equality under the law but proof that America was sliding down a slippery slope of atheism, communism, and depravity. All made worse by subsequent rulings from the bench that legalized homosexuality, abortion, birth control, interracial marriage, and of course desegregation, voting rights, and other civil rights rulings.

But to the NAE, America's economic values and system were as essential to preserving "the American Way" and an American Christian nation as moral and social issues. Capitalism and Christianity went hand in hand. So communism and the welfare state were common epithets used to label any type of social programs that benefited the poor or minorities as un-American and ungodly. With its strong emphasis on individualism and individual responsibility, the NAE cast programs like welfare, food stamps, or Section Eight as in direct opposition to personal responsibility and repentance of sin. White Evangelicals saw poverty, ignorance, crime, violence, and/or addiction as solely attributable to bad life choices, laziness, and criminal tendencies. In this context, social programs only made matters worse by encouraging laziness, immorality, and materialism. In 1967, the NAE passed a resolution stating:

> As evangelical Christians we greatly deplore the evidences of accommodation to the ideology supportive of Communism observable in America today . . . we see this in the evidence of a growing disregard for the rights of the private sector and the growing acceptance of the doctrine "from each according to his ability, to each according to his need," not as a Christian principle but as a fixed economic law . . . In such a time as this, a society which once was described as Christian should resist every form of atheistic Communism.

This resolution coupled Christianity and capitalism. Where White Evangelicals had been at the forefront of many social reform movements just a half-century earlier, now the NAE took on the task of maintaining and defending free market economy as an integral part of American Christian faith. The NAE's Office of Public Affairs held seminars to inform and train White Evangelicals on the encroaching influences of communism. Of course everything from civil rights legislation to raising the minimum wage was lumped under that encroachment!

A minority of NAE members did challenge the apparent individualistic focus of the NAE and argued for the place of social reform within Evangelicalism. After all, the Bible states clearly what

God thinks about those who focus only on evangelism while ignoring the physical needs of those being preached to:

> Suppose a brother or a sister is without clothes and daily food. If one of you says to them, "Go in peace; keep warm and well fed," but does nothing about their physical needs, what good is it? In the same way, faith by itself, if it is not accompanied by action, is dead. But someone will say, "You have faith; I have deeds." Show me your faith without deeds, and I will show you my faith by my deeds. (James 2:15-18)

The same New Testament epistle goes on to make clear that social concerns and maintaining Christlike character are both part of Christian faith.

> Religion that God our Father accepts as pure and faultless is this: to **look after orphans and widows in their distress** and to **keep oneself from being polluted by the world**. (James 1:27)

By the 1960s and 1970s, there was strong division in the NAE between the centrality of individual repentance/salvation and the social implications of the gospel. This division reflected larger fractures among White Evangelicals nationwide. This was the height of the Civil Rights Movement and desegregation. White Evangelicals in the South were fighting tooth and nail in this time period against the very social reforms many Northern Evangelicals had come to support.

In 1967, the NAE released its twenty-fifth anniversary manifesto, reaffirming "a mission of evangelism to salvation" as "the sole and sufficient preoccupation of the church." This didn't preclude individual members from participating in social action so long as the purpose and approach of such activities was carefully articulated, emphasizing the role of evangelism and spiritual growth rather than broad social change.

One such example can be seen in the NAE's partnership with the National Negro Evangelical Association (NNEA) and its Commission on Social Concern during the mid-1960s. The partnership involved two ministry efforts: a pulpit exchange between NAE and NNEA churches and an evangelism campaign in a low-income, overwhelmingly Black and Hispanic area of southern Los Angeles. This was a time when the news was dominated by race riots and generalized social unrest in Los Angeles characterized by Whites as "Communists and Black Nationalist groups."

A generic letter from the NAE chair made clear that race or other controversial issues should not be addressed during this pulpit exchange. Both White and Black pastors agreed that the symbolism of the exchange was at least a small step toward racial reconciliation during the most segregated time in America—Sunday mornings. For the evangelism campaign, a joint committee of NAE and NNEA planned tract-distribution, youth rallies, prayer, and gospel broadcasts by Rev. Howard Jones, the "Negro Associate Evangelist" of the Billy Graham Evangelical Association.

Both activities focused primarily on improving race relations through symbolic acts of reconciliation and individual evangelism rather than any type of ongoing community-impact partnership that addressed the actual social concerns spawning race riots and unrest. This reflected the NAE's suspicion of social action and core ideology of social change only through the individual. Like Graham, many NAE members feared that sustained attention to social justice threatened a needed focus on individual sin and salvation.

The NAE's political leanings reflected this orientation. While the NAE often denied any official involvement in politics, it urged members to act individually. The NAE's Office of Public Affairs offered seminars that encouraged White Evangelicals to pursue careers in federal service in order to influence public policy. This direction from Evangelical organizations like the NAE and others solidified public perceptions of White Evangelicals as implacable social conservatives invested in issues reflecting free economy and morality rather than addressing any systemic societal ills.

What can be noted here is that White Evangelicals had no problem inserting themselves into the political process to legislate issues of personal morality in which they were invested like abortion, homosexuality, and school prayer. But they decried as "liberal" any organized movements to deal with social injustice such as segregation, poverty, police brutality and unequal incarceration of minorities, social and educational programs designed to provide a path out of poverty, or even a livable minimum wage and work programs so the poor could support themselves rather than resort to welfare or food stamps.

By the 1970s, "social concern" had become an epithet among many concerned White Evangelicals synonymous with communism and un-Americanism. At best it was tainted by the ill-advised, erroneous policies of secular liberals or well-intentioned but misguided Christians. The definition of Evangelicalism was boiled down to a negative. If every social evil stemmed from personal sin, then saving souls should be the sole and sufficient purpose of evangelism, and evangelism was therefore the sole and sufficient purpose of the evangelical. This simplified the defining and identification of the "other" as anyone who did not adhere to the "true" definition of Evangelicalism.

But this recasting Evangelicalism in the mythic construct of White American patriotism, capitalism, and dominance not only alienated African Americans as a community but the Black Evangelicals the NAE was trying to bring into the fold. The broad Evangelical presumption of America's origins as a Christian nation inherently celebrated White American history while ignoring fatal flaws such as slavery and ongoing racism. By promoting and ultimately requiring that all "true" Evangelicals buy into this myth and its political implications, White Evangelicals leaders and institutions alienated racial minorities whose personal and collective histories testified to a different America. An America that oppressed African Americans and maintained White privilege.

Black Evangelicals offered an alternate reading of American history to challenge the complacency of White Evangelicalism. In their national story, the atrocities endured by Blacks revealed the self-interested motivations of White Americans from the nation's birth to the present day. Far from a grand myth of faithful Christians seeking freedom and equality, America's story was one of sinners striving for power.

NATIONAL BLACK EVANGELICAL ASSOCIATION

The National Black Evangelical Association, or NBEA, was established in 1963 with similar theologically conservative doctrine and practices as the NAE. Its foundational purpose wasn't to be separate from White Evangelicals but to focus on the needs and evangelism of African-American communities, an area they felt the larger NAE had neglected.

Black Evangelicalism was not uniform as to social policies. Most of its original leadership had been educated at White Bible colleges and seminaries, and many were ambivalent about taking any active role in social reforms that might offend the dominant White Evangelical movement or challenge the emphasis on individual sin and salvation they had been taught in White Evangelical schools.

That changed with the Civil Rights Movement as the overt crackdown on Black civil liberties and the prominent role of Black churches in the Civil Rights Movement could no longer be ignored. Activist Black Evangelicals argued that African American Christians needed to move beyond White paternalism and form their own institutions and leadership. A more conservative element argued that such a stance was divisive and that Black Evangelicals needed to be more conciliatory toward the much large White Evangelical NAE.

In the end, the NBEA remained conservative in basic Bible-believing theology while more active and outspoken on social issues than its White counterpart. Its original vision statement reflects this.

Although our ministry is holistic in scope—dealing with every aspect of life and relating to all classes of people, we nevertheless, like our Lord Jesus, accept the particular call to minister to the needs of the poor, the powerless, and the oppressed, especially as related to Black people.

A major difference of the NBEA was an absence of patriotic rhetoric espousing American exceptionalism common to the NAE and other White Evangelical institutions and a focus on providing practical responses to Black poverty and social injustice, not just in the United States but globally. This included a statement of solidarity in 1977 with Black South Africans in opposing apartheid and other expressions of support to oppressed peoples seeking justice and freedom.

This in complete contrast in the same time period to White Evangelical support of Republican administrations installing and empowering dictatorships such as Mobutu in the Congo, Pinochet in Chile, Stroessner in Paraguay, Ferdinand Marcos in the Philippines, Noriega in Panama, Somoza in Nicaragua, and Mubarak in Egypt. Not to mention arming and supporting repressive nations that persecuted Christians such as Saudi Arabia and Pakistan. Each with the sole justification that these dictators were favorable to Republican corporate business interests, especially in the exploitation of oil and mineral rights in those nations. Clearly "Christian American" principles such as democracy and freedom could once again be ignored so long as those being oppressed were Black and Brown people groups.

Among top NBEA leaders were two prominent Black evangelists, Tom Skinner and William Pannell. Both wrote powerful autobiographical narratives during the late 1960s not dissimilar to other Black consciousness-raising narratives written by Civil Rights legends like Martin Luther King, John Lewis, and Malcolm X all the way back to more historical narratives like the autobiographies of Booker T. Washington, Frederick Douglass, and Sojourner Truth.

Unique to Skinner and Pannell was that they wrote to a dual audience of both Black and White Americans. Both authors hoped to awaken White Evangelicals to the plight of African-Americans brothers and sisters in Christ and correct false impressions of "Christian America." They spoke up against White Evangelical rhetoric of American exceptionalism by exposing the racial disparities that made such discourse so offensive to African Americans. Ultimately, both Skinner and Pannell hoped their corrective autobiographical narratives would illustrate the collective neglect of the Evangelical church and its misguided defense of a mythical past it did not fully understand.

TOM SKINNER

Tom Skinner's memoirs, *Black and Free* (1968) and *How Black is The Gospel?* (1970), narrate his life from teenaged Harlem gang leader to evangelist. Much like the well-known Nicki Cruz/David Wilkerson story *The Cross and the Switchblade*, Skinner's narrative follows the familiar Christian conversion story. While getting ready for a gang fight, Skinner heard the gospel message on the radio and gave his heart and life to Christ.

But little else of his narrative would be comfortable for White readers. Skinner described the Christianity he'd been exposed to from childhood as an upwardly-mobile white-man's religion.

> The impression I had of Jesus from the white society that preached about Him was as the defender of the American system, president of the New York Stock Exchange, head of the Pentagon, chairman of the National Republican Committee—a flag-waving, patriotic American.

Skinner dedicated *Black and Free* to "the more than twenty-two million Negroes in this country, many of them frustrated because they were born black" but also to "the evangelical Christian church in America" that had "failed desperately" to address racism and poverty.

White Evangelicals were by their very numbers and religious beliefs the demographic in the best position to spearhead racial reconciliation. To Skinner, they had failed to do so precisely because they were blinded by the myth of Christian America. White Evangelicals like Billy Graham equated Christianity and American patriotism as almost synonymous. Skinner spoke of a Jesus who would address the White Evangelical establishment with the same outrage Jesus had addressed the Pharisees, calling them "brood of vipers" and "blind guides" for their religious hypocrisy (see Matthew 23; Luke 11:37-54).

Whites in the 1960s routinely blamed African Americans for the social ills in their communities. Skinner laid out American history from an African-American perspective, arguing that these problems were consequences of systematic discrimination and racial violence all the way from the nation's inception. He jarred his reader with graphic descriptions of inner-city poverty such as the anguished cry of a Black mother whose new-born infant was killed by rats or a fire caused by faulty wiring. He painted vividly the atrocities African Americans had endured over the centuries—rape, lynching, familial separation, economic discrimination—and their lasting impact on the Black community.

He also laid out clearly how the inescapable link between White dominance and the church perpetuated the social systems oppressing African Americans. Like nineteenth century Black abolitionist Frederick Douglass, Skinner proclaimed his deep faith in Jesus Christ while excoriating the hypocrisy of White Evangelicals who claimed to believe the gospel while neglecting to see the humanity of its Black citizens. Douglass had once stated:

I love the pure, peaceable, and impartial Christianity of Christ. I therefore hate the corrupt, slaveholding, women-whipping, cradle-plundering, partial, and hypocritical Christianity of this land. Indeed, I can see no reason but the most deceitful one for calling the religion of this land Christian.

To Skinner, the worst of White Evangelical hypocrisy was how it alienated Black Americans from Christ. White Evangelicals prioritized gaining new believers. Yet like Skinner before he came to Christ, many Blacks were understandably suspicious of a Christ presented in the image of an Anglo-Saxon Protestant suburbanite. Such a Christ would hardly love, much less die for Black people. While White Evangelicals believed their role in the nation should be one of maintaining the status quo and even turning back the clock, Skinner advocated that Evangelicals should address social injustices and strive to correct them because these were basic principles of the Kingdom of God. He validated his support as a Black Evangelical minister for the Black social justice movements of his time by saying:

I am not involved in the Black revolution simply because it is Black. I am involved in the Black revolution because it is Christ.

WILLIAM PANNELL

A contemporary of Tom Skinner, William Pannell partnered with Tom Skinner Ministries in 1968 and later became a Professor of Evangelism and Director of Black Church Studies at Fuller Theological

Seminary. Unlike Skinner, Pannell's memoir *My Friend, the Enemy* focused more on the challenges of being Black within White Evangelical institutions. He had an insider's perspective of White Evangelical culture since he had attended Fort Wayne Bible College in Indiana, which was overwhelmingly White Evangelical.

Pannell first realized the profound difference of his Blackness at FWBC when informed he couldn't date like his White friends (FWBC did not permit interracial dating, and there were virtually no Black female students). He was also told that as a Black man he would not likely find employment as a minister or missionary in most Evangelical ministries. Seeing the everyday struggles of African Americans living in poverty, Pannell realized he could no longer preach the standard White Evangelical Christianity he'd been taught at FWBC that blended the gospel with American patriotism, capitalism, and the Republican party. In one powerfully scathing statement, William Pannell sums up:

Scriptural quotations about the end time and the spirit of the age fail to soothe a breaking spirit when one views children looting a neighborhood store for a paltry bag of potato chips. But what would my White brother know of this? He taught me to sing "Take the world But Give Me Jesus." I took Jesus. He took the world and then voted right-wing to insure his property rights.

CHAPTER ELEVEN

TRUMPISM AND

WHITE EVANGELICALS

In 2016, Donald Trump won the presidential election with overwhelming Christian evangelical support. Commentators have struggled to explain how a president who scorns traditional Christian values—as seen in his many affairs, divorces, shady business practices, and close personal friendship with now-arrested sex-traffickers like Jeffrey Epstein and Ghislaine Maxwell—has the overwhelming support of White Evangelicals. Trump himself has famously boasted that he could shoot someone in the middle of Fifth Avenue and not lose his Evangelical base.

Sadly, the answer is simple—hypocrisy. Not so long ago (make that prior to the Republican primaries of 2016!), White Evangelicals still insisted that good moral character, honesty, and sexual faithfulness in marriage were fundamental in choosing political leaders. During the Clinton presidency, White Evangelicals repeatedly claimed that any political leader found guilty of personal moral failing was no longer fit to lead the nation. This was the reason behind impeachment proceedings over allegations of Clinton's sexual impropriety with a White House intern.

A poll prior to 2016 conducted by the Public Religion Research Institute and Religion News Service found that sixty percent of White Evangelicals agreed that a public official found to have committed immorality in their personal life could not be trusted to carry out their duties ethically in their public and professional life. In an identical poll taken in October 2016 after release of the infamous "Access Hollywood" tape, where Trump boasts how easy it is to sexually assault women when you are rich and famous, the number of White Evangelicals who agreed with the prior statement dropped to twenty percent. Data from the Cooperative Congressional Election Study after the 2018 midterm elections found that the percentage of White Evangelicals who believed politicians should be held accountable for personal acts of immorality or unethical behavior had dropped further to 16.5 percent.

These figures changed further if polling questions were posed related directly to Clinton or Trump. Of all demographics polled, White Evangelicals were most likely to change their response depending on which politician was referenced. Only six percent of White Evangelicals queried about Trump responded that elected officials who behaved immorally in private could not be trusted to act ethically in their professional life. Twenty-seven percent of those questioned where Clinton's name was mentioned responded that such a person could not be trusted. In short, party loyalty was the driving force as to whether or not a politician should be held accountable for immoral or dishonest behavior.

Meanwhile, Trump's dishonesty and downright lying has become so brazen that it has created its own vocabulary. A number of national and international fact-checking institutions have documented more than twenty thousand false public statements from Trump since he took office. What is worse is the accelerating rate of lies. It took a hundred days in office to reach five hundred documented lies at a rate of five a day. It took almost two and a half years to reach ten thousand with a spiraling average of twenty-three public misstatements a day. But it took less than fourteen months to reach the twenty-thousand marker on July 9, 2020, with sixty-three documented on-camera mistruths in one day.

Many of Trump's misstatements include vicious lies, accusations, and conspiracy theories about political opponents or anyone attempting to tell truth that contradicts Trump's own narrative. This discounts an entire other genre of easily disprovable claims involving himself—i.e., that he is the smartest, healthiest, most successful, and in general best at everything on the planet, now and throughout history, including as president. Which adds narcissism, name-calling, and just plain mean-spirited bullying to the character flaws White Evangelicals have decided are no longer a problem in their elected officials.

That Trump lies is hardly surprising. Trump has been infamous for decades for lying, corrupt business practices, even such pettiness as calling in fake press interviews under an alias to praise himself. It is impossible to objectively examine decades of Trump's own words on tape and camera and not see the obvious—that he is and always has been a congenital liar. Ask any White Evangelical five years ago to make an assessment of Donald Trump's character and immoral, adulterous, untrustworthy, selfish, narcissistic, greedy, and materialistic would have been typical adjectives.

How did that change to powerful White Evangelical leaders like Franklin Graham calling Trump "a man of God"? Or James Dobson excusing public faults with "well, he is just a baby Christian"? Or multimillionaire prosperity gospel televangelist Paula White (and long-time personal friend of Trump) claiming she personally led Trump to being "born again" during the 2016 primary season? A claim Trump himself has never confirmed, despite the advantage this would give him with his White Evangelical base. It seems that even for additional votes, Trump can't with a straight face verbalize an actual claim that he's given his life to Jesus, repented of his sins, and been born again.

Nor has this supposed new "baby Christian" ever given evidence of "born again" faith. He neither prays, attends church, nor demonstrates any interest in spiritual matters except as part of campaigning events to his White Evangelical base. Certainly, he has shown no change in behavior or speech or repentance of wrong-doing that would bolster claims of being transformed by the redeeming work of the Holy Spirit. On the contrary, he has routinely claimed he's done nothing in his life that needs forgiveness or repentance.

His White Evangelical supporters don't deny that he lies. They have simply come up with new terms for it: "Trump hyperbole . . . He exaggerates to make a point . . . It's just the way he talks."

But such a double standard would seem to only be excusable if the liar is a Republican. Can we forget the years of hyped conspiracy theories when Hillary Clinton read off the CIA's own talking points and current data assessment within twenty-four hours of the Benghazi tragedy? The only differentiation between that statement and the ultimate intelligence findings were whether the cause of the attack on Ambassador Stephens was anger over a video circulating that mocked

Mohammed or because the trip to Benghazi had been scheduled on the anniversary of 9/11.

Neither of which changed the core reality that the militias who'd worked with Stephens to overthrow the Libyan dictator Ghaddafi turned on him without notice. Nor was any suggestion even made of wrong-doing by the State Department. Yet Republicans and White Evangelicals spent years claiming that the difference between public statements right after event and findings months later were "proof" that Hillary Clinton was a liar and Benghazi some kind of massive Democrat cover-up.

Now we have a president who changes his claims of fact hourly while his White Evangelical supporters shrug off the lies with the self-interested rationale: "Well, he's on our side so that's all that matters." One top Evangelical supporter of Trump, theologian Wayne Grudem, spelled out his own justification for Trump lies:

> President Trump is often not careful in some of the things he says. He is given to exaggeration. Sometimes he's made a statement after being given inaccurate information. I'm not sure he's ever intentionally affirmed something he knows to be false, which is how I define a lie.

Never intentionally affirmed something he knows is false? When we now have Trump on tape admitting he knew the seriousness of COVID-19 by late January 2020 even as he spent the following months spreading lies that the coronavirus was all a Democrat hoax and would disappear on its own? When he spreads vicious conspiracy theories with zero evidence, not just against Democrat political opposition, but faithful, honest patriotic conservative Republicans who have served their country with honor for decades within law enforcement, the military, or State Department simply for telling the truth about what they knew of Trump actions and speech?

In August 2020, Grudem reiterated his support of Trump when asked if there was anything Trump could do or say to lose Grudem's support, including the lies and misconduct that emerged during the impeachment hearings. Grudem's response:

> I would stop supporting him if he began to favor higher taxes, more government regulation, a weaker military, open borders, judges who believed in a "living Constitution," extended abortion rights, restrictions on freedom of religion, hostility toward Israel . . .

Hostility toward Israel, restrictions on religious freedom, and expanded abortion rights have not been on the agenda of *either* political party. In fact, one reality White Evangelical Republicans seem to want to ignore is the steady decline in the abortion rate or that it is currently *lower* than before it was decriminalized in Roe vs. Wade.

Which boils down to the sad truth that Grudem's standards for supporting Trump have no connection to biblical morality but simply echo standard White dominance economic and political positions of big military and low taxes (itself an oxymoron only possible by gutting spending on social needs) along with keeping immigrants out and deregulating industry so powerful Republican business interests aren't hampered by environmental or community-impact concerns.

In other words, the very basis of supporting Trump is not based on anything remotely Evangelical, much less biblical, but on economic self-interest and fear of the "other." I.e., those Black and Brown immigrants and refugees who now outnumber more palatable immigrants from White nations (just ask Trump!)

The moral of the story here is that White Evangelicals are hypocrites when they claim to be concerned about family values and the moral fabric of society. They only care about moral and biblical standards when they can use their beliefs as a weapon against the political opposition. So long as a Republican is in the White House, they are happy to turn a blind eye to moral failings. What is also clear is that White Evangelicals have absolutely no right to judge the rest of America when their own house is in such a state of moral disorder.

Much has been said and entire books written over just why White Evangelicals have so passionately embraced a candidate like Trump over more moral, religious, and certainly better-behaved Republican candidates like Jeb Bush, Ted Cruz, Mario Rubio, Rick Santorum, or in fact virtually every other Republican candidate who ran for president in 2016. Here are just a few of the overall conclusions:

- Rising fear and anger toward both immigrants and the growing indigenous population of non-Whites, along with interracial marriage, that threatens White numerical and political dominance.

- A feeling of victimhood and economic anxiety among many White working-class males and to a lesser degree females who feel they are in danger of losing their jobs and livelihoods to "outsiders" (i.e., people of color, immigrants, etc.).

- A paranoia and fear that the dominant White European culture is being replaced and subsumed by an influx of other cultures from Brown and Black nations due to both legal and illegal immigration.

- A stoking of "anti-communism" fears that links everything from affordable health care and raising the minimum wage to Black Lives Matter protests as communist plots while European style "socialism"—i.e., national health care, unions, minimum wage, and anti-poverty programs is touted as a slippery slope toward making America a communist nation.

- An even great fear that immigrants from nations not historically Christian pose a major threat to Christian religion and religious freedoms in the United States. Above all, Muslims. Many White Evangelical leaders such as Franklin Graham, Robert Jeffress, and Jerry Falwell have argued strongly that Islam and Islamic law are the biggest threats to the nation.

- A stoking of fears about crime rates, violence, and social unrest as being solely the purview of Blacks and Browns. This despite the reality that violent crime, much like abortion, has declined sharply in the last twenty-five years, between fifty and seventy percent depending on which data base is considered.

- The historic merge of Big Business and corporate capitalism with White Evangelicalism, a union that since the early twentieth century has seen major donations from Big Business to Evangelical institutions and causes in return for Evangelical leaders preaching from the pulpit a gospel of individual salvation hand in hand with free enterprise while railing against higher taxes, government regulation, and organized labor as "communist" plots. The close ties between White Evangelicals and Republican corporate business interests remains to the present day.

- And finally, a constantly stoked outrage that a "liberal" judiciary should judicate from the bench societal changes White Evangelicals had long enforced legislatively—whether segregation, Black Codes, Jim Crow, interracial marriage, or more directly moral concerns such as the criminalization of abortion and homosexuality.

All of which goes a long way to explain White Evangelical support for a wealthy White businessman committed to unbridled and unregulated acquisition of wealth and lowering taxes on the 1% and corporations. Who shares their fear of the "other." Who is shameless at using disinformation to stoke fear and anger against a non-existent "tidal wave" of criminal, violent illegal Black and Brown he claims will destroy White America without Trump as savior. Who is willing to lay aside his own lifetime liberal stances on abortion and homosexuality to give lip service to a pro-life, pro-family platform without making any attempt to actually legislate such issues, despite have control of both House and Senate for much of his term.

And of course the reason even reluctant and doubtful White Evangelicals continue to support Trump and are willing to ignore the kind of ungodly behavior and speech that would get a five-year-old kicked out of Sunday School. I.e., Trump's commitment to stack the judiciary at every level from local to the Supreme Court with judges committed to the Republican and White Evangelical platform.

Jerry Falwell Jr., president until recently of Liberty University, one the largest and most influential White Evangelical universities, and one of the first Evangelical leaders to endorse Trump for president, has repeatedly made statements that true Christians should elect more leaders like Donald Trump, not despite his bad behavior but because of it. In one tweet, Falwell urged:

Conservatives [and] Christians need to stop electing "nice guys. They might make great Christian leaders but the US needs street fighters like [Donald Trump] at every level of government [because] the liberal fascists Dems are playing for keeps [and] many Republicans leaders are a bunch of wimps!

Perhaps it should be no surprise that even during the writing of this book and lead-up to the 2020 election, Falwell's own hypocrisy, immorality, and lying have been exposed—as well as an ulterior motive for supporting Trump. Shortly before Falwell endorsed Trump, Trump's personal lawyer and fixer Michael Cohen "fixed" an embarrassing affair involving racy pictures of Falwell's wife, a 22-year-old Miami pool boy, and a 1.8 million dollar "business loan" to said pool boy.

After years of denying any wrong-doing and insisting rumors of sexual misconduct related to said pool boy and the bizarre business loan were Democrat lies and conspiracies, Falwell has finally been caught red-handed and forced to admit the ugly truths of a seven-year-long sordid sexual affair, payoffs, and coverups. Not to mention the suspicious timing of pledging his support and that of his huge Christian university empire just as he was being conveniently helped by Trump's own "fixer" (ironically, the same time period it turns out Michael Cohen was "fixing" a $130,000 payoff on Trump's behalf to a porn star!).

Turns out this wasn't about Falwell believing Trump really shared Falwell's White Evangelical beliefs and moral standards. It was about Falwell sharing Trump's penchant for immorality, lying, coverup, amassing personal wealth, partying, and hypocritical lip service to religious faith!

Regardless of who wins the upcoming election, the only too critical question has been asked whether the overwhelming White Evangelical unadulterated support for Trump and condoning his behavior may allow them to "gain the whole world" but "lose their own soul" (Mark 8:36). It has yet to be seen the full impact of this hypocrisy on the credibility and witness of the White Evangelical movement in the United States and globally.

But already the impact can be seen in the alienation and hurt between Black and Brown Christians and their White Evangelical brothers and sisters in Christ.

It can be seen in the younger generation of Americans leaving any Christian affiliation in droves and rejecting what they see as the hypocritical divide between the biblical truths of love, grace, mercy, and compassion their elders claim to espouse and what they are actually seeing in the treatment of refugees, immigrants, minorities, the poor, and the disenfranchised.

It can be seen in the increasing division, not just in the nation and communities but families as political differences have been ratcheted up to a "righteous war" where terms like "the Dems" and "the libs" are used with the same level of hate and contempt once reserved for enemy nations like "the Japs" and "the Huns." Where any wavering in support for Trump elicits questioning of the very salvation of brothers and sisters in Christ with top Evangelical leaders like Franklin Graham, Paula White, and Jerry Falwell suggesting that those who don't vote for Trump are in danger of hell fire.

It can be seen in the stunned reaction of the global body of Christ as they watch and listen to Trump's divisive, abusive, demeaning rhetoric and behavior to "the least of these" (Matthew 25:40-45). Or lauding dictators like Kim Jong-Un, Putin, and Saudi crown prince Mohammed bin Salman while bashing the leaders of staunch democratic allies.

It can be seen in the disbelief of Black and Brown Christians in other nations as they watch their fellow Christians in the White Evangelical American church raise no voice in opposition to putting immigrant children in cages, separating refugee children from parents, or banning refugees (many of them Christian) solely because their nation of origin is majority-Muslim. As they see their White Evangelical brothers and sisters filling their social media posts with countless debunked conspiracy theories designed only to increase division.

The American White Evangelical church, on the forefront of global missions and evangelism around the world for the last two centuries, has lost its historical dominance and moral high-ground within a global Evangelical movement in which they are now a minority to Black and Brown national church movements. Not because the global Evangelical movement is not appreciative for past benefits of White Evangelical missions and evangelism. But because they too see White Evangelical adulation of Trump as both hypocritical and in direct contradiction of what the American White Evangelical church has claimed to stand for around the world.

There are White Evangelical leaders who warn that unbridled support for Trump could come at a cost. But sadly, a recent poll conducted by the Public Religion Research Institute placed White Evangelical approval of President Donald Trump at seventy-five percent, higher than when he was elected, while over eighty percent say they will vote for Trump regardless of anything he does and says. White Evangelical leaders who have spoken out for accountability on Trump have been savaged by their peers, as evidenced by the attacks from Franklin Graham and other White Evangelical leaders on the editors of *Christianity Today* for running an op-ed questioning Trump's moral fitness for presidential office.

Bottom line, to a large percentage of people inside and outside the United States, inside and outside the Evangelical movement, inside and outside Christianity itself, the White Evangelical American church is not perceived as loving, compassionate, kind, or Christlike but just the opposite—as angry, fearmongering, racist, materialistic, and concerned more for their own economic self-interests than living out the gospel of Jesus Christ.

This does not mean that every individual White Evangelical falls into such a characterization—any more than every Black and Brown American is an inner-city gang member or junkie living off welfare. On the contrary, there are millions of White Evangelicals who truly love God and desire to follow God's call to love their neighbor—even those who are Black and Brown. Many are reaching out individually in areas of social concern and justice. Many wish they could make all the unpleasantness of racial division just go away but feel helpless on how to make a stand.

But as a corporate body, the White Evangelical church in America has been co-opted by a political agenda focused far more on selfish ambition and a desire for temporal power than any biblical definition of "Make America Great Again." Its drumbeat for White American exceptionalism, a mythical Christian Golden Age, the correlating of

White Evangelicalism with White prosperity, capitalism, and economic power while spreading fear of Blacks and Browns, blaming the oppressed for their social ills, sounding the alarm of "communism" at every move toward social or civic reform, has changed little in rhetoric since the days of slavery, the Confederacy, Black Codes, Jim Crow, or the civil rights battle. Jesus addressed the religious establishment of His day with stern words, warning:

> This people honors me with their lips, but their heart is far from me; in vain do they worship me, teaching as doctrines the commandments of men" (Matthew 15:9, ESV).

Too much of American White Evangelicalism is not and never has been biblical doctrine but simply raising to the level of God's inspired word the selfish commandments and self-interests of men. Nor is it only White Evangelicals to whom a finger can be pointed. We are all guilty of considering our own interests, needs, family, and community first. White, Black, Brown, if we are followers of Jesus Christ, we must be willing to be crucified with Christ (Galatians 2:20), to deny ourselves and take up Christ's cross (Luke 9:23), and to put into practice the true commandments and doctrines of our Savior like the following:

> Do nothing out of selfish ambition or vain conceit. Rather, in humility value others above yourselves, not looking to your own interests but each of you to the interests of the others. (Philippians 2:3-4)

Let no one seek his own good, but the good of his neighbor. (1 Corinthians 10:24)

So in everything, do to others what you would have them do to you, for this sums up the Law and the Prophets. (Matthew 7:12)

My brothers and sisters . . . serve one another humbly in love. For the entire law is fulfilled in keeping this one command: "Love your neighbor as yourself." (Galatians 5:13-14)

My dear White brothers and sisters, please hear my heart! You tell us as Black Christians that if we do not vote for a man who clearly despises us that we are not Christians. Paula White, millionaire pastor of a predominately Black congregation who uses their tithes and offerings to pay for her $3.5 million condominium in Trump Towers, preaches this from her pulpit!

I know God. I hear His voice. I want to do His will. Trump is the one whose actions are inconsistent with being a child of God. He has said he has no reason to seek forgiveness from God. He has claimed to have done more for Christians than Jesus Christ. He has consistently shown his blatant racism in word, actions, and policies against Black and Brown people.

This is not of God! It breaks our hearts as Black and Brown children of God. How can we embrace this man? Why do you want to subject us to this pain? Don't you know that God is the one that has made us and will cause us to stand? That we are quite as capable of hearing from God in who to vote for as Paula White, Franklin Graham, or Jerry Falwell?

Please do not be brainwashed. Seek for yourself and do not assume you know what God has spoken to our hearts. Or that if we are truly listening to God, we will be hearing what serves your own political interests.

CHAPTER TWELVE

A BIBLICAL RESPONSE

So what is a biblical response to these issues? It boils down to one—love. Love is what breaks down the barriers between people groups, Black and White, rich and poor, privileged and disadvantaged, the powerful and the week. Jesus stated clearly that love is God's greatest commandment. Love of God and love of our neighbor. All our neighbors of all colors, stripes, and creeds.

Hearing that Jesus had silenced the Sadducees, the Pharisees got together. One of them, an expert in the law, tested him with this question: "Teacher, which is the greatest commandment in the Law?" Jesus replied: "'Love the Lord your God with all your heart and with all your soul and with all your mind.' This is the first and greatest commandment. And the second is like it: 'Love your neighbor as yourself.' All the Law and the Prophets hang on these two commandments." (Matthew 22:34-40)

Our faith as Christians, as Evangelicals, should be centered upon love. Conversely, Scripture is clear how God views those who claim to be His followers but do not love others.

> Dear friends, let us love one another, for love comes from God. Everyone who loves has been born of God and knows God. Whoever does not love does not know God, because God is love . . . Whoever claims to love God yet hates a brother or sister is a liar. For whoever does not love their brother and sister, whom they have seen, cannot love God, whom they have not seen. And he has given us this command: Anyone who loves God must also love their brother and sister. (1 John 4:7-8, 20-21)

> If I speak in the tongues of men or of angels, but do not have love, I am only a resounding gong or a clanging cymbal. If I have the gift of prophecy and can fathom all mysteries and all knowledge, and if I have a faith that can move mountains, but do not have love, I am nothing. If I give all I possess to the poor and give over my body to hardship that I may boast, but do not have love, I gain nothing. (1 Corinthians 13:1-13)

Jesus as the example of perfect love. But love is not what Blacks and Browns are seeing or feeling from White Christians in America. White Christianity has sinned. It sinned when it used the power of a state church and church-controlled aristocracy to oppress its own people for centuries in Europe. It sinned when it preached that non-Whites were not made in God's image so could be enslaved with impunity. It sinned when in the name of Christian faith it built White Christian empires around the world on the backs of Blacks and Browns treated as second-class humans in their own nations. It sinned when it built a nation in America dedicated to ideals of freedom—for Whites only.

This is not to deny countless White Christian individuals and communities who have selflessly loved and served others. Just as many notable Black Christian leaders have responded with compassionate love even while being victimized by oppressive White systems of authority. Leaders such as Frederick Douglass, Sojourner Truth, Dr. Martin Luther King Jr., John Lewis and so many other Black Christ-followers have preached peace, love, and kindness even while standing for truth and justice in the face of White persecution and oppression.

This is also not to deny that Blacks and Brown are also sinners who must repent of their own individual and community sins. But it is not Blacks and Browns who continue to dominate America as a nation and the body of Christ as an American church. As your Black Evangelical sister in Christ, I ask with deep love and sorrow that you as White Evangelical Americans humbly listen to us whom White Christianity has devastated—both Black Christians and Black non-Christians alike.

If true racial reconciliation is to happen inside and outside the American church, then the White American Church must specifically repent, admitting both our pain and the horrific legacy of White Christianity within the United States. A legacy disguised under the myth of a Golden Age Christian nation even while much of White Christianity's outreach ministry within the United States and around the world is devoted to addressing the very problems it had a large part in creating. Systemic racism. Unjust legal systems. Economic inequality. Biased and unequal educational institutions. Unfair wages. Political corruption. Poverty. And so many other evils.

What are some specific ways in which a start can be made on the path toward genuine Christian racial reconciliation? The following are only a few suggestions of many that could be made. But they all start with first acknowledging there is a problem and praying repentantly for a change of heart that allows White American Christians to see at least darkly and as a vague reflection in a mirror (1 Corinthians 13:12) through the eyes and hearts of their Black and Brown brothers and sisters.

As an Individual

1. First, educate yourself as to the historical reality of racism in America, including its very founding as a free nation.

A majority of White Americans don't believe racism continues to exist because they have no knowledge of its true role in American history as well as in general European colonial conquests globally. The recommended reading list in Appendix B at the end of this book is a good place to start in learning the full truth left out of much teaching of history in White American education.

2. Second, be willing to challenge exhibitions you personally observe of racism and/or injustice.

Whether in your family, friends, community, elected officials, or even church leadership, be willing to call others out for expressions of racism or White Supremacy. This can be frightening and intimidating since wrong-doers rarely appreciate being confronted. But we are called to speak the truth of God's Word in love (Ephesians 4:15). Show courage in taking a stand against evil.

3. Take deliberate steps to engage with people outside your own racial identity.

Many Whites will claim racism isn't an issue because their own communities are almost exclusively White. And many Whites reacting with contempt or resentment toward minority groups have never actually interacted with people from that group. It is hard to hate others once you've actually gotten to know them as a person, met their families, learned their culture, listened to their grievances and point of view. A well-known saying that sums this up is that "you can't understand someone until you've walked a mile in their shoes." But well-known nineteenth century American author Mark Twain perhaps sums this point up even better.

Travel is fatal to prejudice, bigotry, and narrow-mindedness, and many of our [American White] people need it sorely on these accounts. Broad, wholesome, charitable views of men and things cannot be acquired by vegetating in one little corner of the earth all one's lifetime . . . you never saw a bigoted, opinionated, stubborn, narrow-minded, self-conceited, almighty mean man in your life but he had stuck in one place since he was born and thought God made the world and dyspepsia and bile for his especial comfort and satisfaction.

Traveling outside your own comfort zone doesn't necessarily mean getting on a plane, train, bus, car, or even a ship as in Twain's day, to some other region or country. But few communities however small are monochromatic these days, and getting to truly know other cultures and peoples right in your own area is still just as fatal to prejudice and racism. Consider visiting a non-White church, joining a mixed-race Bible study, volunteering with that community outreach to Syrian or Central Asian refugees minority children, or just inviting a family of another ethnicity over for Sunday dinner.

4. Stop enabling racism and divisiveness in the public arena and public speech.

This includes calling for accountability and civility in political leaders who use their position and power to stir up hate and fear of "others." To name-call, bully, and demean their opponents. To incite their followers to violence. There is no place in the Christian faith for hateful chants like "send them/her back . . . lock them/her up." What do you think the next generation is learning when they watch Christians—their parents, pastors, church leaders—approving and even applauding such behavior?

5. Become directly involved in issues of social reform and justice.

This might include something as socially risky as actually joining a peaceful protest in support of refugees, treatment of immigrants, accountability from law enforcement. Or it may be starting with volunteering to help new refugees with English lessons, orientation to American culture, chauffeuring, and other community services. Or volunteering with the Boys and Girls Club, Big Brothers or Sisters, and other outreach programs to disadvantaged and minority children.

AS A CHURCH CONGREGATION

1. First, develop an open and honest repentance.

Repentance is imperative as a White American church for historic complicity in slavery, racism, oppression since the settling and founding of America. This may mean an actual public service where past sins of racism and oppression as a congregation and community are openly admitted and repented of. This is especially urgent in communities and churches that actively supported Black Codes, Jim Crow, the KKK, segregation, and other overt racism.

2. Second, consider developing as a congregation an ongoing relationship with a specific non-White community, neighborhood, or people group who face oppression/ poverty/need.

Many churches carry out short-term community outreaches or projects with their youth groups or as a church. But there is often little lasting impact on either the community or church because volunteers simply come to carry out a specific task, go home feeling good about doing good, but haven't spent the time to actually get to know those being targeted.

This should be more than just establishing a food bank where those in need must come to you. Get to know the community leaders and ask how you can best help as a church. Some simple effective outreaches have been a joint church/community youth outreach. Or adopting a specific refugee group in your area to volunteer with long-term. A Bible Club/children's outreach into a specific minority housing project. A children and youth sports mentoring program. Partnering with Black and other ethnic churches in ongoing community outreach and ministry programs to disadvantaged neighborhoods.

3. Third, develop partnerships with church congregations of other ethnicities/races.

This is not necessarily a Black and White exchange. Along with Black congregations, any single community may have Hispanic, Chinese, Vietnamese, Arabic, Korean, Burmese, or other Christian ethnic churches, many of them refugee communities. Along with partnering for community outreach, consider simply visiting each other's congregations, planning joint worship services, celebrations showcasing each other's traditions and foods, church camps and retreats, reciprocal joint youth outings and sports events, women's and men's events.

If your congregation isn't willing to reach out to other people groups, consider starting with the small step of guest speakers to bring that cross-cultural experience to your congregation. Bottom line, it is hard to hate and fear people once you get to know them as brothers and sisters in Christ, friends, partners in ministry.

4. Fourth, actively investigate how your church can encourage multiracial attendance.

If you belong to a megachurch that already has many nationalities, speak to the non-dominant-race members, asking their input on how to better foster strong interracial relations and congregational life. Ask their input as well on political views that may differ sharply from the dominant White membership due to differing life, cultural, and historical experiences. Even if political views remain very different, simply understanding where the member of another ethnicity is coming from can foster understanding and acceptance of a different point of view. In fact, I hope and pray that will be one outcome of reading this book.

5. Fifth, stop promoting from the pulpit political leaders who align themselves with White Privilege and fan the flames of racism and hate of "others."

Above all, stop preaching damnation and threat of hell to brothers and sisters in Christ who in good conscience cannot support the same candidates or political party as fellow church members. This isn't to suggest White Christians must vote for politicians who don't represent their own economic and social interests any more than Blacks and Browns should be expected to do so. Simply that it is imperative such a vote be recognized for what it is—a vote for one's personal, family, and people group's self-interests—rather than making that vote the mark of spirituality/salvation and excoriating those who vote otherwise.

The political advice of the great eighteenth century British Evangelical preacher and evangelist John Wesley, recorded in his personal journal less than two years before the American Declaration of Independence was signed, remains as true today:

> October 6, 1774: I met those of our society who had votes in the ensuing election, and advised them: 1) To vote, without fee or reward, for the person they judged most worthy. 2) To speak no evil of the person they voted against; 3) To take care their spirits were not sharpened against those that voted on the other side.

What powerful advice—and, sadly, little practiced either in today's White Evangelical church or from the political stage by the politicians they support. It is easy to point out that there is plenty of negative rhetoric from the political opposition, some approaching the ugliness that pours from Trump's lips every time he addresses the nation. But that is not the issue here, as the apostle Paul pointed out to the early Church almost two thousand years ago.

> I wrote to you in my letter not to associate with sexually immoral people—not at all meaning the people of this world who are immoral, or the greedy and swindlers, or idolaters. In that case you would have to leave this world. But now I am writing to you that you must not associate with anyone who claims to be a brother or sister but is sexually immoral or greedy, an idolater or slanderer, a drunkard or swindler. Do not even eat with such people. What business is it of mine to judge those outside the

church? Are you not to judge those inside? God will judge
those outside. (1 Corinthians 5:9-13a)

We are not called to point fingers at an unsaved world and insist
like quarrelling children that we don't have to behave with Christlike
character until those we denounce as unbelievers behave with
Christlike behavior. We are called to "clean up our own house" and to
judge the behavior and attitudes of those within the Church, not
without.

If there is one overt impact that the election of Donald Trump has
had on the White American church that is crystal clear to onlookers, it
is that his example of public name-calling, bullying, and
hate/race/fear/conspiracy-mongering has somehow given tacit
permission to White Christians to say and do as Trump says and does
in a way that would never have been acceptable within White
Evangelical circles before the Trump era. Too often, White Trump
supporters in and out of the church can be heard publicly saying
statements such as "He says what we've all wanted to say . . . he
expresses what we all feel and didn't dare say . . . Finally, someone is
speaking up for us."

How sad that such expressions of hate, fear, and contempt were
what too many White Christians have been feeling and wanting to say
inside. How even sadder that the election of a man too many claim as
their appointed savior from God has freed them to utter such
unloving, ungodly sentiments. Brothers and sisters, this is not from
God!

6. Sixth and finally, preach from the pulpit what God has to say about loving others, social justice, racial equality, caring for the "others" among us.

At the end of this book is an appendix of Bible passages that speak of God's commands on how to treat the foreigner, orphan, poor, widowed, and disadvantaged. This appendix only scratches the surface. Consider a study from the pulpit on what God has to say on fair treatment of workers, the oppression of the poor by the rich, His wrath against religious leaders who use their wealth and power to oppress the poor, needy, and foreigners among them.

Consider also writing up a church vision statement on racial reconciliation and inclusion that unequivocally welcomes all races into your congregation. Post it on your website and church walls. Memorize it as a congregation. Do so in a way that any person of another color, ethnicity, language group, or citizenship will know they are welcome the moment they step foot into your church sanctuary.

This is a moment of crisis, dear White brothers and sisters, not just for the United States of America, but for the American church. We as brothers and sisters in the family of God and body of Christ, White, Black, and Brown, must be on the front lines of loving, serving, and engaging within our communities and nation as Christ commanded us. We must be willing to repent of past wrongs and come together as one Church to continue impacting our nation with the gospel of Jesus Christ.

Not to make America a Christian nation. That is not our job or calling. Our calling is to repent within the Church so that those without will indeed know we are Christians by our love (John 13:35). Our calling is to make America a nation so filled with Christians totally dedicated to loving God and loving their neighbor that the influence of the real "Christian nation"—God's Church—will spill over into every aspect of our daily lives, communities, politics, and churches.

In conclusion, the only way to "Make America Great Again" is to renounce hypocrisy, turn from racism, repent of past injustice, and return to the values laid down in God's Word, the Bible, from the creation of the world. Not as a White America versus a Black and Brown America. Not as a White American Church versus a Black and Brown American Church. But as one America, one Church, one body, and one family under God. Only then will the United States of America ever be that shining light to a watching world that will bring glory to God our Father (Matthew 5:14-16).

Dear White brothers and sisters, if I have been bluntly honest in these pages, please believe me that it is out of love and because God has laid so strongly on my heart this message. I started this book with a Bible passage God gave me when, like the prophet Ezekiel, God called me to be a watchman on the city wall to raise the alarm for my nation. A watchman who sees the sword coming and does not raise the alarm and warn the people will have the blood of those people on his hands (Ezekiel 33:1-8, ESV). But God gave Ezekiel another more hopeful promise as His watchman:

> Son of man, I have made you a watchman for the people of Israel; so, hear the word I speak and give them warning from me . . . If you do warn the wicked person and they do not turn from their wickedness or from their evil ways, they will die for their sin; but you will have saved yourself . . . **But if you do warn the righteous person not to sin and they do**

not sin, they will surely live because they took warning, and you will have saved yourself. (Ezekiel 3:17-21)

Dear White Brothers and Sisters, with much love, tears, pain, and sorrow, I have spoken the warning God laid on my heart. It is my deep prayer and hope that as righteous followers of Jesus Christ you will receive that warning with the love with which it has been given. I pray that you will consider its message with an open heart, listen to the Holy Spirit as to what your response should be, and take action according to God's leading.

We as Black Christians, as Black Evangelicals, are seeking God's face. We are hearing from Him. We love His Word. We are looking for His coming. I plead with you, my White Evangelical brothers and sisters, please embrace us. Stand up for us in your actions and deeds. Do not demand of us that we follow and embrace that which is clearly evil to us in the politics and practices of certain White Republican politicians. Do not allow your Christianity to be weaponized and politicized.

Choose that which is good. Choose Christ and His Word. Take a stand against racism and divisiveness. Stand up for Christ! Stand up for us.

We love you as our sisters and brothers. Please love us back.

Appendix One

Biblical Foundation for Social Action

The Bible, which we as Evangelicals claim to believe as God's Word and to follow as our guide, has much to say on the treatment of the poor, widow, orphan, unemployed, and foreigner among us. Here are just a few passages in which God commands His followers to care for those less advantaged. Yes, this includes individual charity but also clearly applies to organized social programs on a community and nation-wide basis since many of the below commands were given to the people of Israel as laws for their nation.

Leviticus 19:33-34: When a foreigner resides among you in your land, do not mistreat them. The foreigner residing among you must be treated as your native-born.

Love them as yourself, for you were foreigners in Egypt. I am the Lord your God.

Numbers 15:15-16: The community is to have the same rules for you and for the foreigner residing among you; this is a lasting ordinance for the generations to come. You and the foreigner shall be the same before the Lord: The same laws and regulations will apply both to you and to the foreigner residing among you.

Deuteronomy 10:17-19: For the Lord your God is God of gods and Lord of lords, the great God, mighty and awesome, who shows no partiality and accepts no bribes. He defends the cause of the fatherless and the widow, and loves the foreigner residing among you, giving them food and clothing. And you are to love those who are foreigners, for you yourselves were foreigners in Egypt.

Deuteronomy 15: 7-10: If anyone is poor among your fellow Israelites in any of the towns of the land the Lord your God is giving you, do not be hardhearted or tightfisted toward them. Rather, be openhanded . . . Give generously to them and do so without a grudging heart; then because of this the Lord your God will bless you in all your work and in everything you put your hand to.

Deuteronomy 24:17-19: Do not deprive the foreigner or the fatherless of justice, or take the cloak of the widow as a pledge. Remember that you were slaves in Egypt and the

Lord your God redeemed you from there. That is why I command you to do this. When you are harvesting in your field and you overlook a sheaf, do not go back to get it. Leave it for the foreigner, the fatherless and the widow, so that the Lord your God may bless you in all the work of your hands.

Jeremiah 22:3: This is what the Lord says: Do what is just and right. Rescue from the hand of the oppressor the one who has been robbed. Do no wrong or violence to the foreigner, the fatherless or the widow, and do not shed innocent blood in this place.

Zechariah 7:10: Do not oppress the widow or the fatherless, the foreigner or the poor. Do not plot evil against each other.

Malachi 3:5: "So I will come to put you on trial. I will be quick to testify against sorcerers, adulterers and perjurers, against those who defraud laborers of their wages, who oppress the widows and the fatherless, and deprive the foreigners among you of justice, but do not fear me," says the Lord Almighty.

Matthew 7:12: So in everything, do to others what you would have them do to you, for this sums up the Law and the Prophets.

1 John 3:17-18: If anyone has material possessions and sees a brother or sister in need but has no pity on them, how can the love of God be in that person? Dear children, let us not love with words or speech but with actions and in truth.

See also Exodus 22:21; 23:9; Leviticus 23:22; 24:22; 25:35; Isaiah 1:17; Ezekiel 47:21-23; Matthew 25:35; Hebrews 13:2; James 1:27.

APPENDIX TWO

COLLATERAL READING

T he below titles include many of the sources for material referenced in this book and the Ph.D. thesis on which the book is based as well as recommended collateral reading for readers who may want to dig deeper into this topic.

American Bible Society, *The State of the Bible Survey; Barna Group*, 2018.

Baldwin, James. *On Being White' and Other Lies; In Black on White: Black Writers on What It Means to Be White.*

Bonilla-Silva, Eduardo. *Racism Without Racists: Colorblind Ideology; Racism and the Persistence of Racial Inequality in the United States.*

Brown, Charles Ewing. *When the Trumpet Sounded: A History of the Church of God Reformation Movement, Anderson.*

Butcher, James. *Christian Pharisees: The Striking Similarities of America's Conservative Christians and Jesus' Earthly Enemies.*

Carr, Cynthia. *Our Town: A Heartland Lynching, A Haunted Town, and the Hidden History of White America.*

Christerson, Brad, and Michael Emerson. *The Costs of Diversity in Religious Organizations.*

Cone, James H. *Black Theology and Black Power.*

Dyer, Richard. *The Matter of White Supremacy; In Theories of Race and Racism.*

Emerson, Michael O., and Rodney M. Woo. *People of the Dream: Multiracial Congregations in the United States.*

Emerson, Michael, and Christian Smith. *Divided By Faith, Evangelical Religion and the Problem of Race in America.*

Frankenberg, Ruth. *The Mirage of an Unmarked White Supremacy; In Making and Unmaking of White Supremacy*, edited by Birgit Brander Rasmussen

Ginzburg, Ralph. *100 Years of Lynchings.* Baltimore: Black Classic.

Goldenberg, David M. *The Curse of Ham: Race and Slavery in Early Judaism.*

Haney Lopez, Ian F. White. By Law: *The Legal Construction of Race.*

Harding, Vincent. *There is a River: The Black Struggle for Freedom in America.*

Harvey, Jennifer. *White Supremacy and Morality: Pursuing Racial Justice Through Reparations and Sovereignty.*

Johnson, Dean. *Critiquing the Soul of White Supremacy and the Spiritualities of Whiteness: Narrative and Everyday Praxis.*

Jones, William R. *Is God a White Racist? A Preamble to Black Theology.*

Kaplan, E. Ann. *The "Look" Returned: Knowledge Production and Constructions of White Supremacy in Humanities Scholarship and Independent Film.*

Kidd, Colin. *The Forging of Races: Race and Scripture in the Protestant Atlantic World.*

Mansfield, Stephen. *Choosing Donald Trump: God, Anger, Hope, and Why Christian Conservatives Supported Trump.*

Nancy, Rochelle Parks-Yancy, and Corinne Post. *White Views of Civil Rights: Color Blindness and Equal Opportunity; In White Out: The Continuing Significance of Racism.*

Powell, Adam A., Nancy R. Branscombe, and Michael T. Schmitt. *Inequality as Ingroup Privilege or Outgroup Disadvantage: The Impact of Group Focus on Collective Culpability of God and Interracial Attitudes.*

Segrest, Mab. *The Souls of White Folks; In the Making and Unmaking of White Supremacy.*

Tranby, Eric, and Douglas Hartmann. *Critical White Supremacy Theories and the Evangelical Race Problem: Extending Emerson and Smith's Divided by Faith.*

Van Ausdale, Debra, and Joe R. Feagin. *The First R: How Children Learn Race and Racism.*

Verter, Bradford. *Furthering the Freedom Struggle: Racial Justice Activism in the Mainline Churches Since the Civil Rights Era; In The Quiet Hand of God.*

Wildman, Stephanie M., and Adriene D. Davis. *Making Systems of Privilege Visible; In Critical White Studies: Looking Behind the Mirror.*

Wilmore, Gayraud S. *Black Religion and Black Radicalism: An Interpretation of the Religious History of African Americans.*

Wu, Frank H. Yellow: *Race in America Beyond Black and White.*

ABOUT THE AUTHOR

Dr. Karen T. Felix-Neal is co-founder and co-pastor with her husband Dr. Rev. Gaylord Neal of *A Higher Dimension Church*, "a church without walls" which teaches and preaches God's Word seven days a week. Ministry focus is on spiritual leadership, discipleship, prayer, and Bible reading. Felix holds a PhD in Christian Organizational Leadership and is a CFO (Chief Financial Officer) and business development consultant. Visit her at her webpage **www.drfelixthewatchman.com**.

Made in the USA
Middletown, DE
16 October 2020